THE HOCKEY PLAY BOOK

Teaching Hockey Systems

Michael A. Smith

FIREFLY BOOKS

Cataloguing-in-Publication Data

Smith, Michael A.

The hockey play book : teaching hockey systems

ISBN 1-55209-050-7

1. Hockey – Coaching.
2. Hockey – Training.
I. Title.

GV848.25.S65   1996   796.962′2   C96-930945-7

A FIREFLY BOOK

Published by
Firefly Books Ltd.
3680 Victoria Park Avenue
Willowdale, Ontario
Canada M2H 3K1

Published in the U.S. by
Firefly Books (U.S.) Inc.
P.O. Box 1338, Ellicott Station
Buffalo, New York 14205

Produced by
Bookmakers Press Inc.
12 Pine Street
Kingston, Ontario K7K 1W1

Design by
Roberta Voteary

Printed and bound in Canada by
Friesens
Altona, Manitoba

Printed on acid-free paper

Front cover photograph
© David Prichard/First Light

Legend

RD	Right Defenseman
LD	Left Defenseman
RW	Right Wing
LW	Left Wing
C	Center
X_1	Right Defenseman
X_2	Left Defenseman
X_3	Right Wing
X_4	Left Wing
X_5	Center
⋯▶	Pass (arrow shows direction)
⟶	Player movement (arrow shows direction)
----◄	Shot (arrow shows direction)
I	Full Stop
●	Possession of puck
–·–	Point of contact
△	Pylon

CONTENTS

HOCKEY PLAY

INTRODUCTION

HOCKEY IS A GAME PLAYED BY YOUNG ATHLETES AND A GAME IN WHICH youth is not entirely determined by age. NHL players bring the same enthusiasm to the rink as eight-year-olds, and no matter what level the players, it is the coach's responsibility to create an atmosphere and environment that gives shape to that enthusiasm. Games are fun. That is why people of all ages play them.

The techniques explained in these pages are cut-and-dried; the diagrams and text are brief and to the point. Coaches reading this book, however, need to remember that their job is to bring these plays to life and that the lessons contained in this book are intended to channel players' excitement, never to stifle it.

This book focuses on the different systems that are part of hockey. There is no one system, no best system, no secret system. Hockey systems are not complex or difficult to learn, although some, it is true, can be challenging to execute. They do take teamwork, though, and it is part of the coach's job—actually, a major part—to foster an eager and effective team spirit and, once it exists, to orchestrate its actions.

When I started coaching in the early '70s, I thought the road to being a good coach was straight. If I learned A and then B and C, and so on, I would become a skilled coach and know everything I needed to know. But I discovered that the more I learned, the less I knew for sure. What once looked clear and simple often became gray and diffused.

I concluded that a good coach had to become an artist and that the process of guiding a hockey team was subjective. I learned that a good coach must constantly create if he is to enable his players and his team to grow.

The purpose of this book, then, is to provide resources for coaches who are caught up in their own creative efforts. These chapters include different systems for hockey's defensive, offensive and special team situations. Teaching methods and drills are

provided, and the systems run the gamut from the conservative to the aggressive. Some systems are designed specifically for big physical teams or for fast-skating and highly skilled teams or for teams that have both. In this book, there should be a system for every coach.

But here is a warning. Despite the look of this book, hockey is definitely not a game of x's and o's. Diagrams help, but a coach is in trouble if ever he thinks players can learn the game from a chalkboard. It is vital not to make hockey rigid. It is a fast-flowing game with the opportunity for physical confrontation, and it is important for the coach to incorporate both the flow and the physical elements into his plans.

In a sense, the game of hockey resembles jazz. Talents and skills are necessary, but a basic framework is required within which to exercise these abilities. Both jazz and hockey demand improvisation; the individual player doing the extra unexpected bit makes the system work. The individuals play off each other and constantly adjust to one another, and in hockey, just as in jazz, too much planning can ruin everything.

There is no perfect system. Different coaching philosophies emphasize different techniques. Coaches who believe in aggressive, attacking play proceed differently than coaches who believe in a conservative, close-checking approach. Some coaches want aggression in some zones and conservative play in others, and a coach must come to grips with his philosophy of the game before selecting specific systems for play in any one of them.

Once a coach has decided what kind of team he has at his disposal and knows roughly how he wants to proceed, this book can help him lay out his plans. It can help with adjustments to his present techniques, and maybe contains a couple of ideas he hasn't thought of before. Later in the season, when the team is in a slump and enthusiasm is slipping away, perhaps this book can even supply a little of the creative magic that every coach should always be looking for.

SECTION
ONE

DEFENSIVE PLAY

PLAYERS DREAM ABOUT SCORING GOALS AND MAKING THE WINNING PLAY, not playing defense. There is no glory in backchecking, and there is no trophy at the end of each season for the player who most often clears the zone. But defensive play lays the foundation for the offense. It is this seemingly unattractive part of the game that permits a team's dreams to become reality.

The coach must create an atmosphere that gives birth to the team's desire for effective defensive play, and he must teach players to see defensive play as active, not just reactive. Defense becomes fun when the team realizes that success is directly related to its defensive play.

Coaches also need to teach that each successful defensive play is the beginning of an offensive play. Good forechecking forces the puck to be turned over, often for a scoring opportunity. Good neutral zone play creates the opportunity for counter-attack. Good defensive zone play precedes breakouts.

As you look through the chapter on defense, you'll notice that the number of options decreases as the opposition brings the puck up the ice. The reason for this is simple: The closer the other team gets to your net, the less room there is for recovery. The closer he is to his own net, the more specific a player's job becomes and the more disciplined he needs to be.

Defense is largely about grit and determination. Defense discloses character, and coaches have to look for effort and energy and the ability to persist in the direction of the greatest resistance. Once a coach has found defensive players with character, the following systems will work.

DEFENSIVE PLAY

Three things are vital to success—conditioning, fundamentals and working together as a team.

John Wooden
They Call Me Coach

CHAPTER ONE

FORECHECKING

FORECHECKING IS THE PROCESS OF ATTACKING THE OPPOSITION IN THE offensive zone and doing so in a way that leads to disruption, which leads to confusion, which leads to chaos, so that your team gains possession of the puck and scores a goal. Forechecking, in other words, is about getting the puck back.

All teams have to be good at forechecking to be successful. Fortunately, there are many forechecking systems to choose from, and no one system is the ultimate. All systems have some degree of flexibility built in, and this means that whatever system a coach chooses, adjustments can be made in preparation for a particular team and even during a game.

The choice of a forechecking system will depend on the coach's philosophy and on the personnel available. Some systems are geared for aggressive, quick-skating teams. Others may fit slower-skating teams that emphasize size and physical play.

An aggressive system, one that relies on the better skating ability of the forechecking team, usually attacks before the opposing players are organized and attempts to prevent them from getting into their positions. A conservative-system attack takes place after the opponents are organized, as they begin to move out of their end, and often at a specific place. Some systems combine the aggressive and conservative philosophies.

Every team should master at least one forechecking system and be able to make changes within that system to address different situations. A conservative emphasis works best to protect a lead; a more aggressive approach may be necessary when attempting to come from behind. Knowledge of more than one approach can be beneficial, but a team has to have mastered its primary system before learning a second.

Above all, forechecking demands hard work. Nothing can replace it. As a coach, you are teaching players to create chaos; encourage them by pointing out that contributing to the other team's chaos is a highly satisfying way to expend their energy.

Standard Triangle

KEY POINTS

The triangle stresses one forward on the puck, a second in position to move in to help the first, and the third in position to backcheck or to move to the slot on offense. The defensemen play a normal position. The system attacks the puck and prepares the team for the neutral zone if the offense clears the zone. The system can be used by both quick-skating and physical teams. This is a good system to introduce to young teams. For older teams, it can serve as a starting point for a new season. It teaches players basic checking and rotation as well as how to read and react to each other.

1. The Standard Triangle forechecking system is easy to teach, with objectives that are simple and direct.

2. It stresses positional play while permitting interaction between the three forwards.

3. It is adaptable to most breakout plays.

4. It stresses pressuring the puck carrier.

5. The primary defensive principle is to prevent the opposition from breaking out 3-on-2.

6. Its execution requires basic checking techniques.

Basic Alignment. The three forwards form a triangle in the offensive zone. Either the puck-side wing (LW) or the first forward in the zone attacks the puck. The Center backs up the LW, and the third forward (RW) is in the slot. The defensemen (LD and RD) take normal positions.

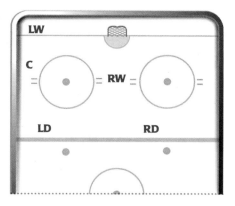

2 The objective is to pressure the puck carrier. The LW moves on X1. The Center positions himself either to move in and help the LW or to stay with X3.

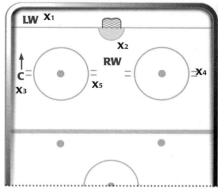

If the LW has two players to contend with (X1 and X5), the Center moves in to help. The LD must be in position to check X3.

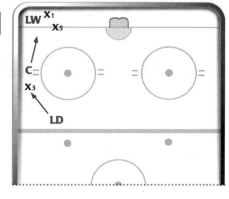

4 If the puck is passed behind the net (X1 to X2), the RW moves in to pressure X2. The Center then moves across to back up the RW, and the LW moves to the slot, and the triangle is reestablished.

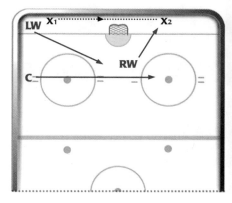

If the puck is passed around the boards to X4, the RD must move in on X4. The LD moves across to cover the RD's position, and the Center pulls back to the LD's position.

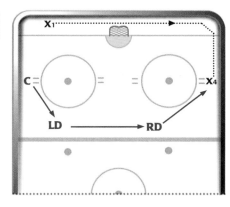

6 This diagram illustrates the triangular positioning of the forwards.

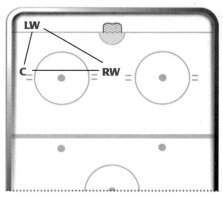

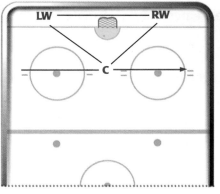

7 This diagram illustrates the triangular configuration, with the Center's position backing up the wings.

1-2-2

KEY POINTS

The 1-2-2 is a conservative system designed to prevent 3-on-2 breakouts and to encourage the opposition to set up deep in its own end. It encourages the opposition's defensemen to carry the puck, and it emphasizes control of the boards. One forward, usually the Center, forces the puck. The other two forwards, usually the wings, play back near the top of the face-off circles. The defensemen play a normal position. It is a good system for teams with big wingers. It stresses basic checking. All teams, at some time, encounter situations that call for a 1-2-2.

1. The 1-2-2 forechecking system is easy to teach, with objectives that are simple and direct.

2. It stresses positional play while permitting basic adjustments and interactions.

3. It is adaptable to most breakout plays.

4. It is positionally balanced: no specific position is the key to the system.

5. It stresses pressuring the puck carrier and checking areas where the puck is likely to go.

6. The primary defensive purpose is to prevent the opposition from breaking out 3-on-2. This is done by keeping both wings back.

7. It is essential for the wings to control the boards.

Basic Alignment. **1**

The Center forechecks the puck carrier, the wings (LW and RW) stay wide, checking the opposition's wings, and the defensemen (LD and RD) play inside the wings.

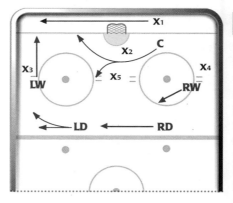

2 The objective of this system is to force the opposition to move the puck to areas covered by the LW and the RW. The Center prevents the opposition from moving up the middle. For instance, the Center checks X1, the LW has the option of moving in if the Center has X1 in check or staying with X3. The LD moves toward the boards and can pinch along the boards. The RD is responsible for the deep middle.

Adjustment to the opposition's breakout. If X5 swings into the corner and X3 comes off the boards straight across the face-off circle, X1 can pass to either X3 or X5. This will flood the area that LW must cover. **3**

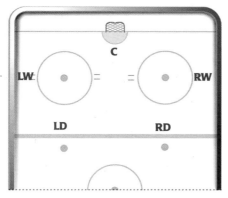

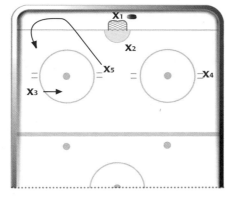

4 The fore-checking unit reacts as follows: The LW picks up X5 in the corner before he swings out of the corner. The Center moves back and to his left, making it difficult for X1 to pass to X3. The RW keeps X4 in check. The LD moves to the boards, and the RD moves to the middle.

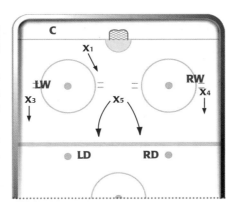

5 If the opposition decides to swing players in both corners, with X2 and X5 swinging into opposite corners, the forechecking unit reacts as follows: The LW picks up X5, the LD picks up X3, the RW picks up X2 in the corner, and the RD picks up X4. The Center stays in front of the net to cover X1. The system calls for man-to-man coverage. If anyone fails to cover his man, the fore-checking breaks down. If it is successful, X1 will normally have to carry the puck. For the most part, the offensive team will not be as successful clearing the zone with a defenseman carrying the puck as it will with the puck being moved to the forwards.

If the Center is beaten, the **6** two wings are in a position to cover the opposition's wings (X3 and X4). This forces the opposition to bring the puck up the middle.

1-4

KEY POINTS

The 1-4 is a conservative system. One forward, usually the Center, pressures the puck. The other two forwards, the wings, play a similar role to that of the defensemen; essentially, four players form a wall across the blue line. The line can move back to the red line as the opposition moves out of the zone. A team often utilizes this system when protecting a lead late in a game. It is frequently used by a team that has significantly less talent. The attack comes as the opposition moves up the ice.

1. The 1-4 forechecking system is easy to teach, with objectives that are simple and direct.

2. It does not stress pressuring the puck carrier in the offensive zone; it essentially gives up the offensive zone.

3. One forward, usually the Center, forechecks the puck or forces the opposition to bring the puck up the wing by positioning himself in the middle of the zone.

4. Two forwards, usually the wings, and the two defensemen work as a unit to form a wall across the ice.

5. The four-man unit has a territorial responsibility.

6. The primary defensive principle is to have four players always in position to defend against the opposition's three forwards.

Basic Alignment. **1** One forward (C) is in the offensive zone. He can either pressure the puck carrier or compel the opposition to go up the boards by shutting off the middle. The other two forwards (LW and RW) form a four-man wall with the defensemen (LD and RD).

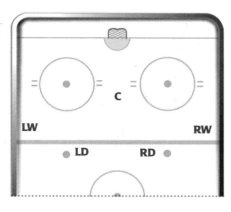

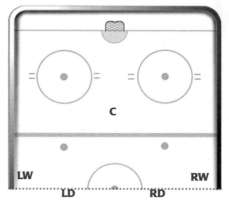

Basic Alignment 2 when the wall is at the red line. This alignment gives away the offensive zone and sets up the forechecking in the neutral zone.

The role of the **3** first forward (C) is to control the middle. He can either move in deep on the puck or stay back and shut down the middle.

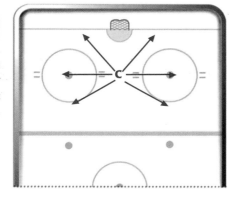

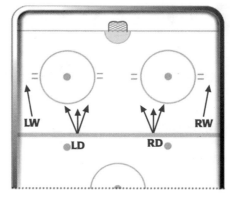

4 The roles for the other four players are basic: The wings cover the boards, and the defensemen cover the middle. Normally, they are not aggressive and do not move deeply into the zone. Rather, their role is to prevent the opposition from advancing the puck through the wall.

The members **5** of the four-man unit react to each other. If the opposition comes up the middle, the LD and the RD play up and the two wings drop back to cover.

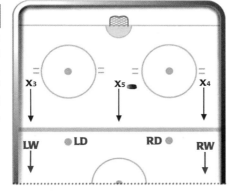

If the **6** opposition comes up the boards, one wing and one defenseman (LW and LD) play up and the other two players (RD and RW) drop back to cover.

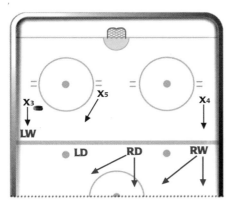

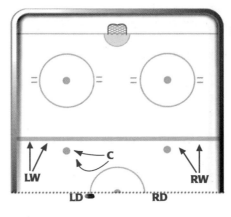

7 When the wall is set up at the red line, the forechecking unit can easily move to the offensive. The wings are in a position to move up quickly, and the Center should already be up.

3-2 Check

KEY POINTS

This is an extremely conservative system. There is really no attack in the offensive zone. The objective is to keep the opposition's forwards in check. The defensemen play a normal position. It allows the opposition's defensemen to carry the puck. The system should be used only by a good checking team. Success is difficult to achieve, since it depends on the defensive forwards to keep the opposition's forwards completely in check.

1. The 3-2 Check system is easy to teach, with objectives that are simple and direct.

2. It does not pressure the puck. It permits the offensive unit free handling of the puck in the offensive zone, particularly in deep.

3. The role of the forwards is to keep the opposition's forwards in complete check.

4. The primary defensive principle is to prevent the opposition's forwards from getting open for a pass. When this system is successful, an opposition defenseman is forced to carry the puck and must beat the defensive defensemen at the red line.

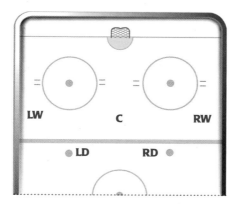

1 **Basic Alignment.**
The three forwards (LW, C and RW) stay high in the offensive zone. The defensemen (LD and RD) play a normal position at the blue line.

Each forward picks up his **2** man—LW and X3, C and X5, and RW and X4— and stays with him.

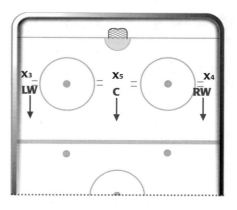

3 If the defensive forwards shut down the opposition's forwards, then the puck-carrying defenseman (X1) must beat the LD and the RD at the red line.

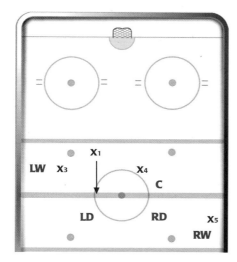

A successful result would **4** have X1 dump the puck forward into his offensive zone. If everyone has his man in check, then the RD is able to get back and retrieve the puck while the LD checks X1.

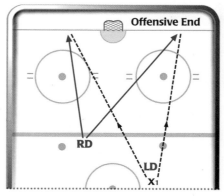

17

1-1-3
Off-Wing
Stay Back

KEY POINTS

This system combines aggressiveness with conservatism. The off-side wing always plays back in position to backcheck and defend against 3-on-2 breakouts. The Center and puck-side wing have an aggressive responsibility to attack the puck. The defensemen play normal positions. To use this system, teams need to have good skating forwards who can anticipate. When successful, it can result in quick counter-attacks on the goal. The conservative forward, the off-side wing, is always in position to move to the slot area.

1. The 1-1-3 forechecking system is easy to teach, with objectives that are simple and direct.

2. It combines positional play with controlled movements.

3. It emphasizes aggressive forechecking but reserves one forward in position to assist the defensemen: two forwards, the Center and the on-side wing, have aggressive forechecking responsibilities, and the off-side wing has a conservative defensive role.

4. It allows forwards the freedom to be innovative when the occasion arises.

5. This system relies on skating and intense concentration by the forwards.

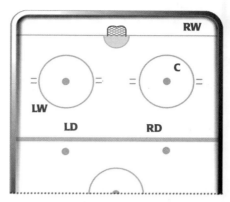

1 **Basic Alignment.** Two forwards, the Center and the puck-side wing (RW), have fore-checking responsibilities. The off-side wing (LW) stays high in the offensive zone. The LW is in a position to move back to play a defensive role or to move to the slot area.

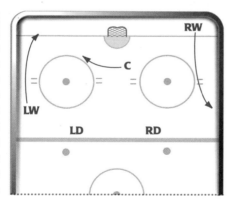

2 The objective is to have the off-side wing (LW) shut down the far board, which forces the opposition to bring the puck up through the fore-checking forwards (C and RW). The first forward (RW) forechecks the puck carrier, and the Center is in a position to assist the RW or to move to the puck if the RW is beaten. The RD is permitted to pinch in, and the LD is responsible for the middle.

3 The forwards often have to rotate. As the play moves from one side to the other, the off-side wing (LW) becomes the forechecker and the puck-side wing (RW) assumes the defensive forward's role. The Center's role remains constant.

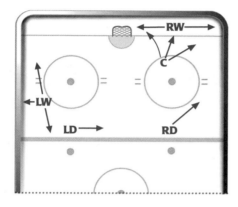

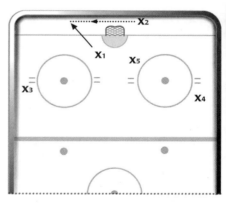

4 Adjustment to the opposition's breakout. If X1 moves to the open area behind the goal line, X2 can pass to him. The objective of this breakout play is to move the puck to an open area (Diagram 5).

5 The LW checks X3 (LW is too high to move to X2 and would be trapped if he did so). The Center moves across the ice, checking X5. The Center then has two options: first, to stay with his check (X5), forcing X1 to carry the puck;

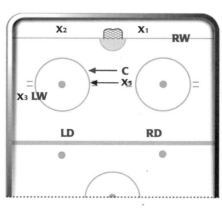

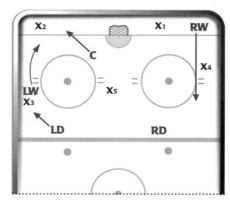

6 or second, to aggressively forecheck X2. If the Center executes the second option, the LW moves in as the second forechecker, the LD may pinch along the boards and the RW drops back to assume the role of the defensive forward.

2-3
One Wing
Always Back

KEY POINTS

This system combines aggressiveness with conservatism. Two forwards, a wing and the Center, constantly attack the puck. The other wing is in a conservative defensive role, always in position to backcheck and to defend against 3-on-2 breakouts. The defensemen play normal positions. The constant roles of the forwards permit set plays to be executed when counterattacking. This system requires forwards who can skate.

1. The 2-3 forechecking system is easy to teach, with objectives that are simple and direct.

2. It combines free, aggressive forechecking by two forwards with a constant defensive role by the third forward.

3. The pressuring forwards have the freedom to be innovative when the occasion arises.

4. This system emphasizes skating, intense concentration and defined roles for the forwards.

Basic Alignment. Two forwards, the RW and the Center, have forechecking responsibilities. The LW always stays high in the offensive zone in a position to become a third defenseman. The defensemen (LD and RD) play shifted toward the right.

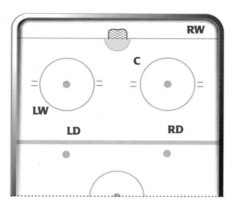

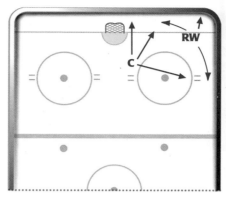

2 The forechecking forwards (RW and C) work in tandem. One forward, usually the first player on the puck, forces the puck. The other forward reacts to the first forward's movements.

When the puck moves to the LW's side, the LW remains in his defensive position. The Center and RW shift their forecheck-ing responsibilities to that side.

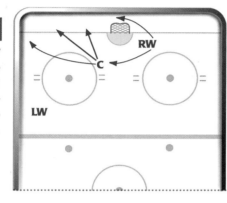

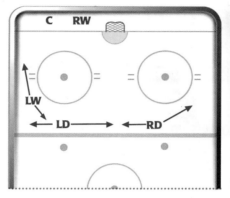

4 With the Center and the RW deep, the LW and the RD have the responsi-bility of defending the boards. They are permitted to pinch if the opportunity arises.

If the RD pinches along the boards, the LW and the LD must cover for him. The LD moves to play the RD's position, and the LW moves to play the LD's position.

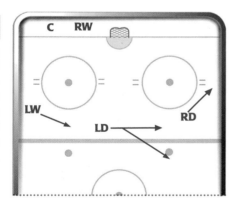

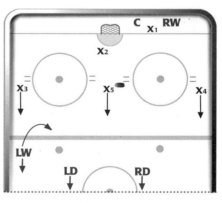

6 The defensive objective of this system is to have three players always in a posi-tion to assume defen-sive roles when the opposition has beaten the two forechecking forwards and has cleared the zone. The LW, LD and RD prevent any 3-on-2 breakouts.

When the forecheckers gain control of the puck, the LW **7** moves to the offense. For example, the RW has the puck, and the LW can move to the slot or deep into the zone. Teams using this system should practice predetermined movements once they gain control of the puck; for example, the RW has the puck, and there are a number of different reactions possible for the other players.

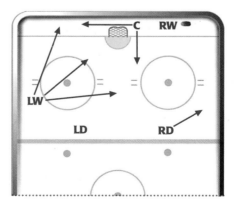

Wings Chase and Center Forechecks

KEY POINTS

This system combines conservatism and aggressiveness. The wings are always moving, getting in position to attack the puck. One wing continues to forecheck while the other pulls back to be in position to backcheck. The Center is a constant forechecker. This is a more flexible variation of the Off-Wing Stay Back system. The defensemen play a normal position. The objective is to force the opposition to move away from the pursuit of the wings. The Center anticipates the direction and is there to pressure the puck. This system needs wings with good skating ability and a Center who is physical.

1. The Wings Chase/Center Forechecks system is a complex one that requires sound interaction between the forwards.

2. Both wings are skating all the time, and their job is to pursue the puck. One forward will always assume a defensive responsibility. This can be flexible; for example, a specific wing can be given this role, or criteria can be established, such as the first wing in will pull back.

3. The Center always forechecks. He must anticipate the area the puck will move to and be there.

4. The skating wings create a deceptive screen. One wing always returns to a defensive role, while it is the Center who actually applies pressure as the second forechecker.

5. The defensemen play a normal position.

6. This system requires forwards with good skating ability.

Basic Alignment. The wings apply pressure with pursuit. The Center is in the middle of the ice and moves to the area where he anticipates offensive movement. The defensemen play a normal position.

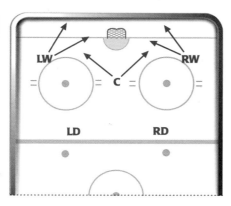

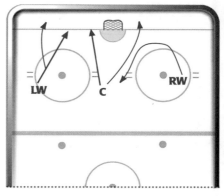

2 If the puck is on the LW's side, he gives pursuit. The Center, anticipating that the puck will end up in the net area, goes there to forecheck. The RW swings back through the middle to assume a defensive role.

In this example, the RW is the defensive wing, and his role is pivotal. His skating and deep positional play put him in a position to discourage the opposition from moving to his side. He is able to move in quickly or pull back to assume a defensive role. The Center, positioned in the middle, keeps the opposition from moving up the ice in that direction.

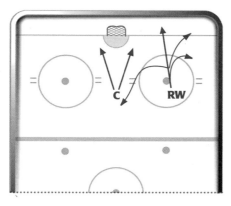

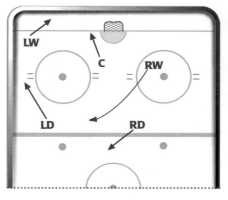

4 The defensemen (LD and RD) are allowed to pinch. In this example, the RW is skating and can cover for the LD, who has pinched in.

5 A second example has the first wing in (LW) assume a defensive role. The LW swings deep and turns back into the middle. He has the option of staying deep. The RW moves in deep to forecheck. The Center again anticipates the direction of the puck and tries to be there. If the LW stays in deep, the Center assumes a defensive position, even though that is not his usual role within this system.

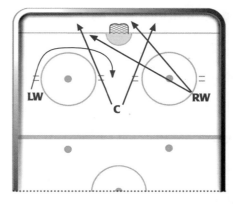

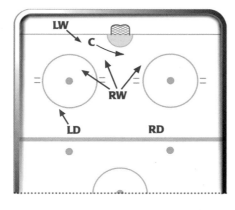

6 When possession of the puck is gained, the RW (from the first example, in Diagram 2) is in the high slot. Since he is moving, he gives some flexibility to the offensive play. The LW and the Center are deep and move to the net area.

2-1-2

KEY POINTS

This is an extremely aggressive system, perfected by the Soviet National teams of the 1980s. It calls for constant pressure on the puck by two forwards. Both defensemen play aggressively, pinching in along the boards. This system, when successful, results in the opposition passing the puck either under intense pressure or blindly in their own end.

The constant pressure forces quick passes, which can be awkward to execute. This system makes it difficult for an opposition player to carry the puck, since the two forwards will pressure him. This system is *not* for all teams. Constant work, speed and anticipation are essential. This system relies on communication between the Center and the defense.

1. The 2-1-2 system is difficult to learn. All the players must thoroughly understand the *defensive* principles.

2. It is a positionally balanced system.

3. It emphasizes the interchanging of positions, which means the players must know the responsibilities of each position.

4. It is a free-flowing system with constant motion, and it emphasizes attacking the opposition at all times and in all areas.

5. It stresses skating and quickness. The ability to play the man is an important asset.

Basic Alignment. **1** Two forwards (either the wings or the first two forwards) are deep. The third forward (usually the Center) plays in the high slot. The two defensemen play wide on the blue line.

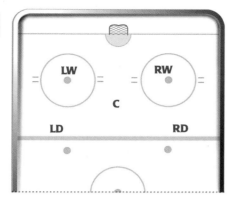

2 The movement of the players permits a great deal of freedom. The structure of the system is symmetrical. The entire zone is covered, with two players always in position to pressure the puck.

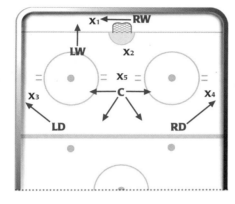

3 The objective is to keep constant pressure on the opposition. The two forecheckers (LW and RW) are aggressive at all times. The third forward (C) backs up the two forecheckers and can become a back-checker or cover for either defenseman, who may pinch along the boards to cover the opposition's wings or the puck. The third forward is also responsible for the middle of the ice and must keep the opposition's center in check.

Adjustment to the opposition's breakout. Constant pressure often **4** forces the opposition to use the boards or to dump the puck to a vacant area. (In this case, the area between the net and the opposite corner is vacant.) If the puck is shot along the boards, the defenseman normally pinches in and the Center moves back to cover the blue line. The defenseman's job is to keep the puck deep in the zone. If the puck gets by the defenseman, the Center is in position to play defense.

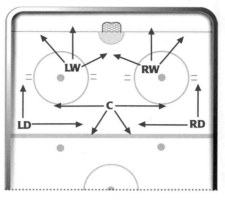

The Center has the option of **5** going to the boards if the opposition's wing is deep. The Center and the two defensemen must communicate to prevent the Center and a defenseman from both pinching in and getting trapped.

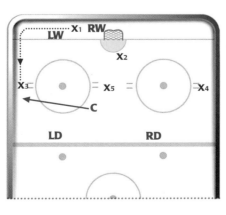

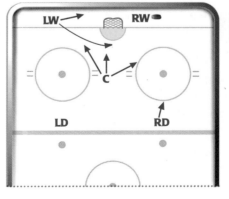

6 If the RW gains control of the puck, the Center is in the high slot and can move in deeper or to either side of the slot. The LW can move deep behind the goal line or to the net. The RD can move to the top of the face-off circle.

Aggressive 2-1-2

KEY POINTS

This is an aggressive system. It places emphasis on forcing the offensive team toward the boards. This system is structured to box the offensive unit in along the boards. Two forwards, the puck-side wing and the Center, are aggressive forecheckers. The two defensemen also have aggressive roles. The off-side wing positions himself either to become a backchecker or to move in and forecheck when the play shifts to his side. This system needs physical forwards.

1. The Aggressive 2-1-2 system is easy to teach, with objectives that are simple and direct.

2. It stresses positional play with explicit roles for its players.

3. The aim is to force the offensive team to the boards so that the forechecking unit is then able to apply pressure using the boards as a boundary.

4. Two forwards, the puck-side wing and the Center, have aggressive forechecking roles.

5. The role of the off-side wing is to backcheck or to move in and forecheck when the play shifts to his side.

6. The defensemen's roles are aggressive. The puck-side defenseman can pinch along the boards. The other defenseman is responsible for the high slot.

7. Physical play along the boards is important.

Basic Alignment. **1** The puck-side wing (LW) and the Center play deep in the zone. The off-side wing (RW) remains high, close to the top of the face-off circle. The LD plays close to the boards. The RD plays farther to the left than normal.

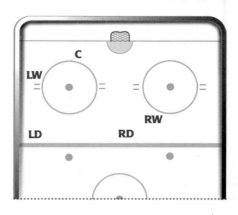

The Center (or the LW if he is **2** the first player in the zone) forces the play toward the boards. The LW positions himself to assist the Center. The LD can pinch in along the boards when the puck or play is there.

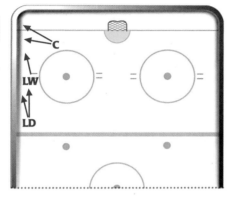

3 The RD's role is to move into the high slot area when the puck or play is there. When the RD moves in, the RW must move back to cover for the RD.

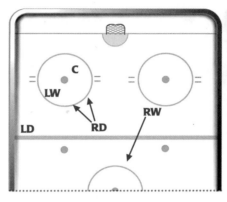

The primary objective of this **4** system is to force the offensive unit to the boards. When this is effective, the offensive team has only one direction to go, directly into the pressure applied by the forechecking unit.

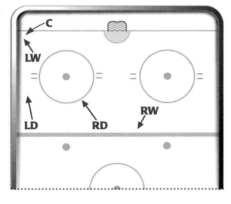

5 The RW is in a position to move quickly to the slot or net area when possession of the puck is gained. For example, if the LW has the puck, the RW moves to the slot and the Center moves to the net.

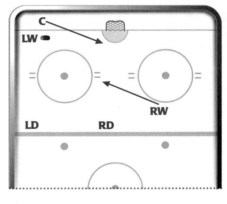

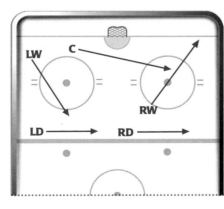

6 When the puck is moved to the opposite corner, the RW moves in to forecheck and the Center moves across the ice to help. The LW moves back high to the top of the face-off circle. The defensemen (LD and RD) shift their positions across the blue line.

One Wing Always Deep

KEY POINTS

This is an aggressive system. One wing, either a specific wing or the off-side wing, always plays deep. The attack is directed toward that wing's side. That wing is always in a position to move quickly to the offense on the counterattack. Aggressive play by the defensemen should be discouraged. Good-skating or physical teams can use this system. The deep wing can be either skilled or physical. Usually, he will have goal-scoring ability.

1. The One Wing Always Deep system is easy to teach, with objectives that are simple and direct.

2. One wing always plays deep in the zone. He is in a position to move to the puck if the flow is in his direction.

3. The first forward (not counting the deep wing) into the zone pressures the puck. The second forward's role is to help the other forechecker or to assume a defensive role, if needed.

4. The defensemen play a conservative role. They do not pinch because the play of the forwards deep in the zone leaves the defense with no one to back them up.

5. When the puck is turned over, the fore-checking unit plays the puck deep because one wing is always there in position to control the puck.

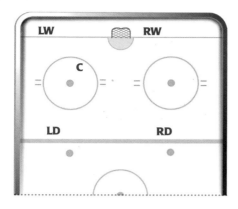

1 **Basic Alignment.** The RW plays deep. This is his task, and he goes directly to the goal line when entering the zone. The first forward (LW) pressures the puck. The other forward (C) backs up the LW. The defensemen (LD and RD) take a normal position on the blue line.

The LW **2** forechecks the puck. The Center is in a position to move in to help or to pull back into a defensive role. Essentially, the LW and the Center work in tandem. If the play stays on the LW's side, the Center will move in to help.

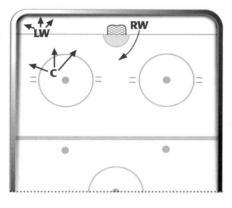

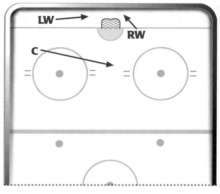

3 If the play moves behind the net, the RW is in position to help the LW pressure the puck. The Center moves across the slot.

The defensemen **4** are conservative. They do not move in on the puck with the three forwards deep, because an unsuccessful attempt at pinching might create a 3-on-1. Having both the LD and the RD back ensures no more than a 3-on-2.

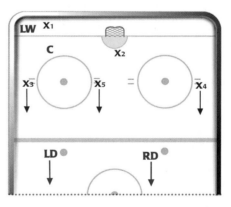

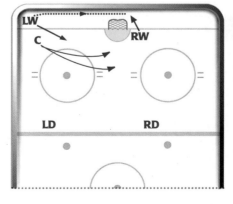

5 When the forechecking unit gains possession of the puck, the RW is already deep and most likely open. The puck should be quickly passed to the RW. For example, if the LW gets the puck, he passes it behind the net to the RW, and the Center goes to the net or the slot.

Aggressive Overload

KEY POINTS

This is an extremely aggressive system. The forwards apply constant pressure. They have no defensive responsibilities; their primary objective is to attack the puck at all times. This system uses both good skating and physical forwards. The defensemen, positioned wider than normal, are permitted to pinch on the puck.

1. The Aggressive Overload system is easy to teach, with objectives that are simple and direct.

2. It is an aggressive system that constantly pressures the puck.

3. The three forwards work together as a unit, and sound interaction between them is essential.

4. The defensemen pinch whenever possible. Their job, when they do pinch, is to get the puck deep into the zone.

5. This system can be effective under specific situations. A small ice surface is useful, but a team trying to overcome a lead may also find it helpful.

6. The pressure comes from exceptional speed or exceptional size; a team with neither should use another system.

FORECHECKING/AGGRESSIVE OVERLOAD

Basic Alignment. 1
The three forwards are in deep (or in the area of the puck). The defensemen play wider than normal on the blue line.

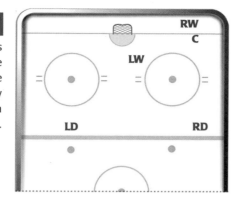

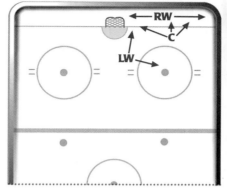

2 The three forwards work together aggressively to pressure the puck. The forwards interact.

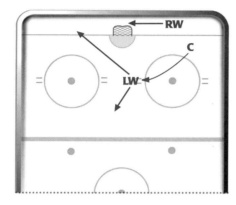

3 One forward should always be higher than the other two. The high forward is in a position to move back, if necessary. Also, the high forward is in position to move to the puck when it moves away from the two deep forwards.

The defensemen are allowed to **4** pinch along the boards. On the puckside, when the RD pinches in, the high forward (LW) moves back toward the blue line.

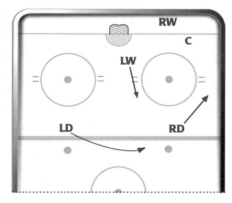

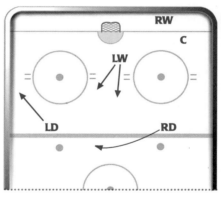

5 When the puck is moved to the far side, the LD pinches in. Again the high forward (LW) moves back toward the blue line. Depending on his position, the LW will move to either the LD or the RD's position.

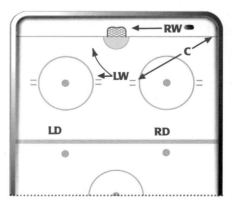

6 When the fore-checking unit gains possession of the puck, the three forwards are already deep and they should apply quick pressure on the net. For example, if the RW has the puck, one or both of the other two forwards (LW and C) should go immediately to the net.

31

3-2 Press

KEY POINTS

This is a highly aggressive system intended for specific situations: face-offs, end of a period or when a certain (weaker) opponent has the puck. The three forwards attack the puck. It is done with the confidence that the three forecheckers will get the puck and produce a scoring opportunity. The defensemen play a normal position with the freedom to join the pressure close to the blue line. All teams can make use of this system.

1. The 3-2 Press system is easy to teach, with objectives that are simple and direct.

2. The primary objective is to have the three forwards pressure the puck simultaneously.

3. This pressure is done with high intensity.

4. The defensemen play a conservative role and remain on the blue line.

5. The forwards apply pressure in an effort to get a quick turnover of the puck and make a direct play on the net.

Basic Alignment. **1**

The three forwards are deep and pressure the puck. The defensemen play a normal position on the blue line.

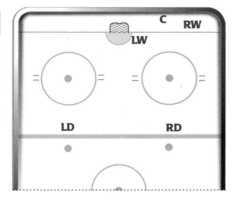

2

Use this system when, for example, X2 (notorious for being poor with the puck) has the puck. Players are instructed ahead of time that when X2 has possession, they are to pressure him in order to create a quick turnover.

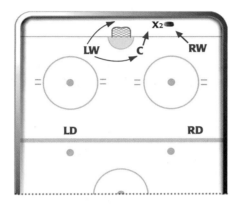

After a turnover, **3** the forwards gain possession of the puck and make a quick and direct play on the net.

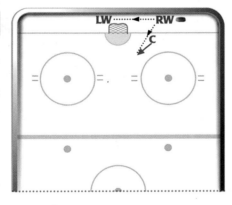

4

A second use for this system is the face-off. The forwards go directly to the puck if the Center loses the draw.

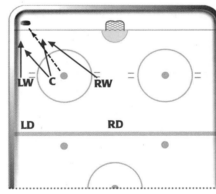

5

Again, a quick and direct play is made on the net after the puck is turned over. The LW has the puck, and the RW and the Center move to the net and deep.

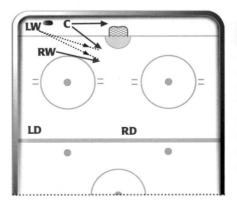

1-2-2
Everything
to the Net

KEY POINTS

This is an aggressive system. The objective is to have one forward attack the puck, with a second always in position to join the attack. Defensemen are permitted to pinch. Two forwards are in position to cover for the defensemen if they pinch. The objective is to direct the attack toward the net. The forechecking pursuit is toward the net. The net becomes an extra forechecker when this is done, crowding the opposition. If the puck is turned over, the players are always directing their play toward the net. This system can be used by all teams.

1. The Everything to the Net approach is complex, with a great deal of interaction between the forwards.

2. It emphasizes pressuring the puck at all times.

3. One player is always on the puck, with a second in position to move in to help.

4. The defensemen pinch whenever possible.

5. The second and third forwards have a dual responsibility to help the forward pressuring the puck and to cover for the defensemen if they pinch along the boards.

6. Interaction between the players is critical.

7. All movement is directed toward the net.

Basic Alignment.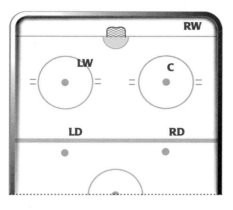
The first forward (RW) moves in deep to pressure the puck. The second and third forwards move in fairly deep to be in position to move toward the puck. The defensemen (LD and RD) take a normal position.

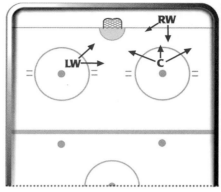
The second and third forwards (LW and C) must always be in a position to move to help the RW. The Center and the RW work together. The LW can move to the net or the slot.

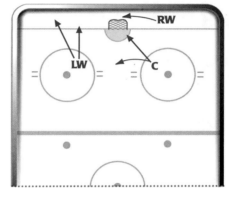
The LW can move in deep to help the RW when the puck is moved behind the net. The Center can move to the net or the slot.

The defensemen are responsible for covering along the boards and are permitted to pinch in. The forwards must cover for the defensemen. The LW moves back toward the blue line to cover for the LD, as does the Center for the RD. The RW moves toward the net because if the defensemen gain control of the puck, they will direct it toward the net.

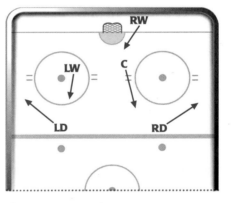

For example, when the LD pinches along the boards, the LW moves to the blue line, the RW to the front of the net and the Center to the slot. If the LD gains control of the puck, he will direct it toward the net or deep behind the net.

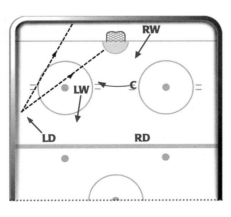

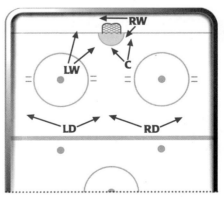
Offensively, this system places the forwards so that two of the three are always in a position to go deep and two of the three are always in a position to go to the slot. The defensemen play normal positions.

3-1-1 Press

KEY POINTS

This is an aggressive system that is used for a face-off. The objective is to attack the puck quickly and move to the net. One defenseman has a defensive responsibility. The other defenseman and three forwards each have a specific area of responsibility in the attack. This system is used at the end of a period or when certain vulnerable opponent players are on the ice. It is used in anticipation that the draw will be won or tied up by the opposition.

1. The 3-1-1 Press system is easy to teach, with objectives that are simple and direct.

2. One defenseman has a defensive role.

3. Three forwards and the second defenseman are aggressive. They each have specific areas to cover.

4. The objective is to gain possession of the puck quickly and make a play on the net.

Basic Alignment. **1**
The RD moves in deep to join the LW, the Center and the RW at the face-off circle.

Each player moves to an **2** assigned area. The RD backs up the forwards, who move ahead from the face-off.

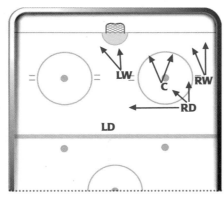

A quick play should be made on **3** the net when the puck is controlled. For example, if the RD gets the puck, the LW is already near the net and the Center and the RW move toward it. The RD shoots quickly or makes a play to the forwards.

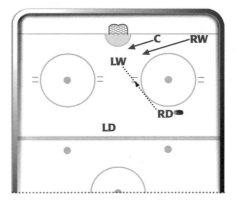

DRILLS

The following drills are examples that can be utilized to teach various components of fore-checking. Drills can be devised to be specific to the different systems.

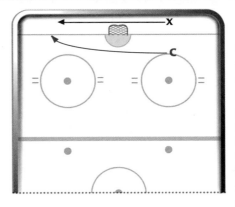

1 **Purpose**: Teach the forwards to check the puck carrier. An offensive player (X) carries the puck along the boards behind the goal line. The Center skates parallel to X, staying a half-stride behind while maintaining the same speed. The Center forces X to go behind the net, prevents him from cutting up the middle and is in a position to check X into the boards and to maintain physical control.

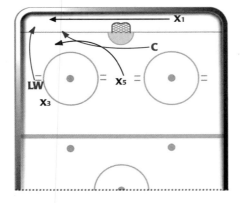

2 **Purpose**: Practice interaction of the Center and a wing. The LW will move in on the puck when the Center has X1 in check. If the LW moves too soon, X3 will become open for a pass from X1. A variation is to add X5 and have him swing into the corner. The LW moves in to check X5, and the Center moves over to cover X3.

Purpose: Teach the defensemen to pinch and control the boards. **3**
The Center will move in to check X and force him to shoot the puck along the boards. The defenseman practices moving to the boards and pinching in to keep the puck in play. The puck carrier should vary the type of clearing shot to help the defenseman learn to control the different shots. A variation is to have the defenseman pinch in on a player taking a pass along the boards.

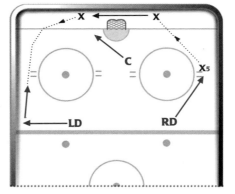

Purpose: Teach the two forecheckers to pressure **4**
the puck carrier. The puck carrier (X) starts a few feet ahead of the first forechecker (RW). The RW forces X to the boards and in the direction of the net. The second forechecker (C) moves in from a different direction. The first forechecker takes the man, and the second forechecker takes the puck.

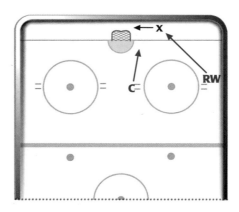

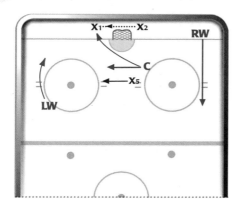

5 **Purpose**: Teach the two forecheckers to react to the opposition's defenseman passing the puck to his partner. The second forechecker (C) reacts to X2's pass to X1 by moving across the ice, keeping X5 in check. The RW pulls back to assume a defensive role. A variation is to have the Center forecheck X1 and the LW move in to become the second forechecker.

Purpose: Teach **6** the interaction of the two defensemen and the off-side wing. The puck carrier (X2) will pass the puck to X4 or shoot the puck along the boards to X4. The RD will either pinch in on X4 or on the puck. The off-side defenseman (LD) moves over to be in position if the play gets by the RD. The off-side wing (LW) moves to the LD's normal position.

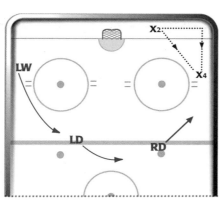

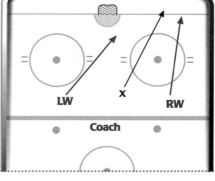

7 **Purpose**: Teach the two fore- checkers to press or attack at all times and to work as a unit. The coach dumps the puck into a corner or along the boards. A defense- man (X) retrieves the puck and attempts to make a play. The two forecheckers, starting at different spots, attack X.

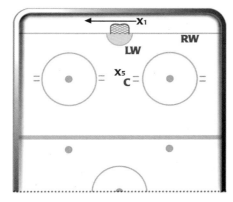

8 **Purpose**: Teach the forwards to interact. Begin with opposition's defenseman (X1) with the puck. Two forecheckers (LW and RW) start 10 feet back. The Center must cover X5 to pre- vent the pass up the middle. Progress to the point that the three forwards inter- change positions. Insert a second defenseman (X2) to teach the fore- checkers to react to passes between X1 and X2. Often, the Center forechecks and one wing assumes the Center's position.

Purpose: Teach the high forward (C) and the two **9** defensemen to interact. This drill has the opposition's defenseman (X1) pass the puck to a wing (X3 or X4). If the wing is high (top of the face-off circle), the defenseman pinches in and the Center moves to the blue line. If the wing is deep, the Center will move to the wing and the defense- man holds the blue line. Emphasize communication in this drill.

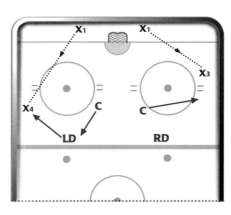

DEFENSIVE PLAY

You will not get far using "old skates"—using old tactics, skills and techniques. What was considered the weapon of the strongest yesterday, today becomes accessible to all.

Anatoli Tarasov
The Road to Olympus

CHAPTER TWO

NEUTRAL ZONE DEFENSE

D EFENSIVE PLAY IN THE NEUTRAL ZONE IS OFTEN OVERLOOKED, AND TOO many coaches are content to tell their players just to "stay in your lanes." But neutral zone defense cannot be reactive; defenders will not be effective in the neutral zone if they wait for their opponents to make mistakes. Defenders in the neutral zone must first attack the puck, then actively and consciously oppose the opposition's attempt to get access to its offensive zone.

Fewer defensive systems are available in the neutral zone because the defending team is now being forced back closer to its own goal and the potential consequences of a mistake have increased. With less room on the ice for recovery, there is less room for flexibility. On the other hand, the opportunities to attack the puck are more specific and often obvious, and it is the attack, often referred to as the "trap," that is critical.

The other thing to keep in mind is that successful neutral zone forechecking will lead directly to an effective offense. The counterattack is part of the neutral zone defense, and the transition from defense to offense needs to be deliberate and well practiced so that it can be executed quickly. Skilled neutral zone forechecking will produce a turnover and transition so quick that the offensive unit will be trapped by the change of possession. Drills that practice the counterattack initiated in the neutral zone are a valuable method for teaching the neutral zone forecheck.

One suggestion useful for all systems in the neutral zone is to divide the zone into five "lanes": two outside, two inner and a middle one. The conservative approach has one player responsible for each lane, and the more aggressive systems have flexible or rotating coverage. In either case, the lane approach serves as a spatial reference tool when defining and teaching responsibilities.

1-2-2

KEY POINTS

This is a conservative system. The wings control the outside lanes while the defensemen control the inner lanes. The Center normally pressures the puck. It is a good system for all teams to be familiar with. Its basic checking tactics, once learned, are invaluable to any system, and all teams will encounter situations during games when the 1-2-2 will be useful. It is an inflexible system that discourages individual innovation. For it to be successful, individual players must be disciplined and control their areas. It helps for each player to have a physical presence in his area. This is a system for teams with big, physical forwards.

1. The 1-2-2 system is easy to teach, with objectives that are simple and direct.

2. It stresses positional play.

3. The wings play a conservative checking style.

4. The defensemen stand up and challenge the offensive unit at the blue line.

5. The Center aggressively forechecks the puck carrier and attempts to force the play to the outside.

6. The system is flexible enough to allow the Center to interchange with the wings.

Basic Alignment. **1**
The wings keep the opposition's wings in check, staying only 3 to 5 feet away and half a stride ahead to prevent them from cutting to the middle. The Center forechecks the puck to force the play to the outside. The defensemen play toward the middle and stand up to force the opposition to make the play in the neutral zone.

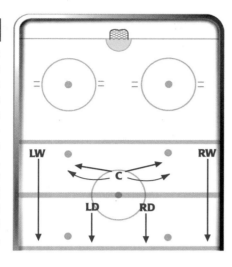

2 The objective of this system is to force the opposition either to turn the puck over in the neutral zone or to dump the puck in. If the puck is dumped in, the wings interfere with their checks, one defenseman picks up the opposing center and the second defenseman retrieves the puck. Note: If the opposition's wings cut to the middle, the defensemen pick them up. The wings stay to the outside, shutting down the outside lanes.

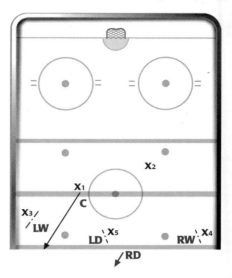

Counterattack. **3**A
If a defenseman (LD) gains control of the puck, the puck-side wing (LW) stays on the boards, the off-side wing (RW) either cuts to the middle or stays on the boards, and the Center swings either way or can set up a pick. The LD has three players to whom he can make a quick outlet pass.

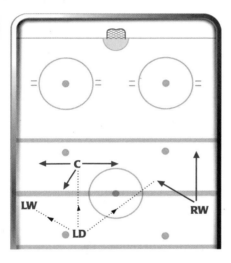

If a wing (LW) **3**B
gains control of the puck, the Center swings to the boards, the off-side wing (RW) either cuts to the middle or stays on the boards, and the puck-side defenseman (LD) can move up into the play. The LW has three players to whom he can make a quick outlet pass.

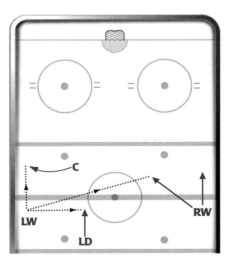

3C If the Center gains control of the puck, because he is the forechecker and up on the play, he must control the puck and allow the wings to get back into the play.

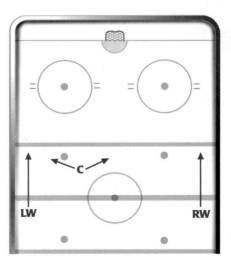

1 - 1 - 3

This system combines conservatism with aggressiveness. The off-side wing's responsibility is to shut down his outside lane. His role, conservative in nature, permits the puck-side defenseman to be aggressive. The system's aggressiveness, the attack, comes from the Center and the puck-side wing. They pressure the puck and, with the assistance of the defenseman, attempt to force turnovers. The 1-1-3, when successful, can become an effective offensive force with its counterattack. This system can be used by teams with good skating ability as well as by teams with big, physical players.

1. The 1-1-3 system is easy to teach, with straightforward objectives.

2. It combines aggressive forechecking and conservative checking.

3. It has one forward (off-side wing) assume a defensive role.

4. The Center and puck-side wing have the option of either one or both pressuring the puck.

5. The three forwards must all understand the system's principles because of their frequent interaction with each other. The defensemen must also understand their interactions with the forwards.

6. The puck-side defenseman stands up at the blue line or in front of it and plays aggressively.

7. The off-side wing and defenseman have defensive roles, which enables the other players to be aggressive and attack the opposition.

Basic Alignment. The off-side wing (LW) plays conservatively, closing down the outside lane. One player, either the Center or puck-side wing, forechecks the puck aggressively. The second forward has the option of attacking the puck or dropping back. If it is the puck-side wing, he covers his wing. If it is the Center, he covers the middle. The off-side defenseman plays conservatively. The puck-side defenseman reacts to the second forward. If the second forward attacks, the defenseman moves wide toward the boards. If the second forward stays back, the defenseman moves either to the middle (if it is the wing who drops back) or to the boards (if it is the Center).

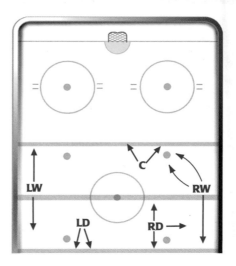

The objective is to pressure the puck carrier using two forwards and the puck-side defenseman. The conservative play of the off-side wing and the defenseman allows the forecheckers to pressure the play in the neutral zone.

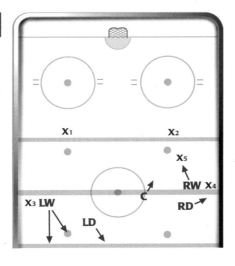

Counterattack. If the puck-side defenseman (RD) gains control of the puck, the off-side wing (LW) moves either straight up the ice or toward the middle, the puck-side wing (RW) goes to the boards and the Center can swing either way. The defenseman has the option of making the outlet pass to any of three players.

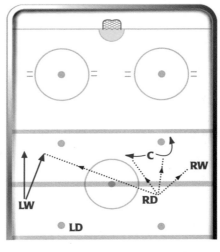

If the puck-side wing (RW) gains control of the puck, the Center swings to the boards or moves directly to the offensive zone; the off-side wing (LW) moves straight up the ice or toward the middle; the puck-side defenseman (RD) can also step up into the play. The RW has three players to whom he can make a quick outlet pass.

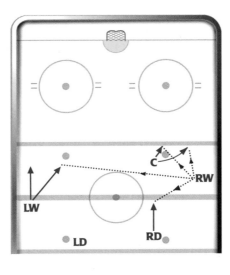

If the Center gains control of the puck, the puck-side wing (RW) moves straight up the ice or to the middle; the off-side wing (LW) moves straight up the ice or to the middle; the puck-side defenseman (RD) can also step up into the play. The Center has three players to whom he can make a quick outlet pass.

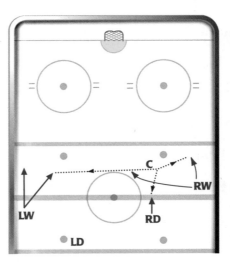

2-1-2

KEY POINTS

This is the extremely aggressive system perfected by the Soviet National teams of the 1980s. It calls for constant pressure by two forwards, usually the wings. The defensemen play wider than normal and are encouraged to pinch along the boards. The Center's responsibilities are to shut down the middle and to back up the defensemen. There is constant motion, with the forwards always skating. Only teams with good skating ability can use this system. The skating forwards allow quick transitions to be made. The constant threat of a counterattack slows down the opponents' offense. This is not a system for all teams. Work, speed and quickness, anticipation and a thorough understanding of the system are essential.

1. The 2-1-2 is a difficult system to learn. The players must thoroughly comprehend its defensive principles.

2. Constant movement is stressed.

3. The wings exert persistent pressure on the puck. The objective is to prevent the opponents from establishing their tempo and style of play in the neutral zone.

4. The defensemen play wide, leaving the Center responsible for the middle. The puck-side defenseman can challenge the play as well as pinch on the boards.

5. The Center is the key player. He reacts to the play of both the wings and the defensemen. He must know the system completely, and his execution permits everyone else to be aggressive.

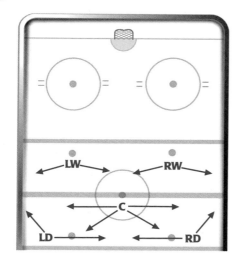

1 **Basic Alignment.**
The two wings play up and pressure the puck. The defensemen play wide and are responsible for the outside lanes. The Center is responsible for the middle. The Center's role is to assist the wings and to back up either defenseman should he pinch or move to the boards.

The objective is to keep constant **2** pressure on the puck. If the puck is forced up the middle, the Center is in position to move in. If the puck is forced to the boards, a defenseman moves in and the Center backs him up. The constant movement encourages the three forwards to interchange with each other. There should always be one forward in a position to cover if a defenseman makes an aggressive move on the puck.

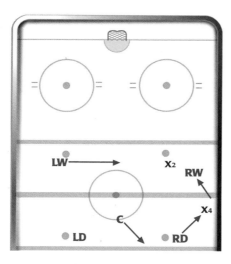

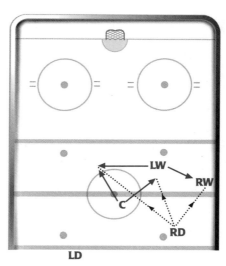

3A **Counterattack.**
If the puck-side defenseman (RD) gains control of the puck, one wing (RW) goes to the boards and the other wing (LW) swings to the far side or sets up a pick. The Center moves either up the ice or across in front of the RD. The RD has three players to whom he can make a quick outlet pass.

The options are more limited if a wing gains control of the puck. The wing, because he is up the ice, can choose to move quickly to the offensive zone with the other wing. The Center will then be the third player to enter the offensive zone.

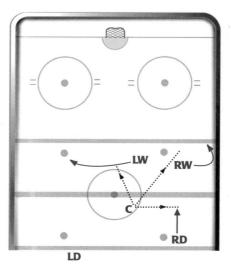

3B If the Center gains control of the puck, one wing (LW) swings across in front of the Center; the other wing (RW) moves toward the boards; the puck-side defenseman (RD) moves up the ice. The Center has three players to whom he can make a quick outlet pass.

DRILLS

The following drills can be utilized to teach various components of neutral zone defense. Drills can also be tailored to the specific systems.

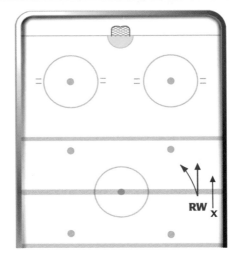

1 **Purpose**: Teach the wings close checking. An offensive forward without the puck skates along the boards, attempting to break for the far end. The defensive player (normally a wing) stays close to the forward, preventing him from getting ahead or cutting to the middle. The checker is allowed to use his body to prevent the offensive forward from cutting to the middle.

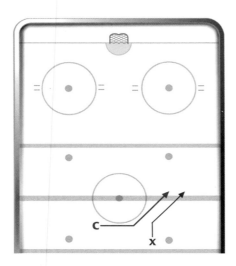

2 **Purpose**: Teach 1-on-1 forechecking. An offensive player skates up the ice with the puck. The forechecker (C) moves to the puck carrier. He must not commit himself and be beaten. His objective is to force the player either to move toward another player who is already in check or to pass to another player who is already in check. The forechecker should always play the man after he has passed the puck.

3 **Purpose**: Teach the defensemen to play the man in open ice. Two cones are placed in the neutral zone to restrict the offensive forward's mobility. The forward carries the puck up the ice, and the defenseman is instructed to make his play by the blue line. The forward, staying within the cones, attempts to beat the defenseman or dump the puck.

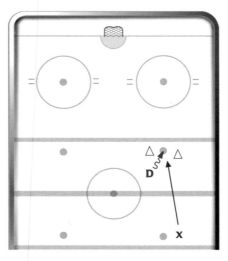

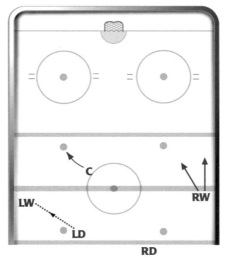

4 **Purpose**: Teach quick transition from defense to offense. The players set up in checking areas. The coach designates which player has gained control of the puck. On the whistle, the players move from defense to offense with the initial outlet pass. Counterattack is crucial, and the players should practice at the different positions to be familiar with all of them.

Purpose: Teach the Center and puck-side wing to work as a coordinated unit. An offensive player (X) moves up the ice with the puck. The Center pressures X toward the puck-side wing (RW), so they together can then double team X. The Center and the RW can also practice interchanging, with the Center going to the boards and RW pressuring X.

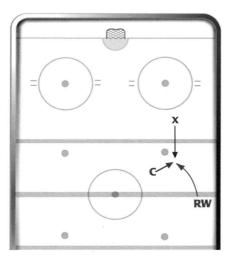

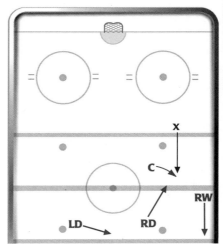

Purpose: Teach the defenseman to stand up in the neutral zone. This drill is the same as Drill 5 with the defenseman added. The puck-side defenseman (RD) stands up at the red line to play the puck carrier (X), who is being pressured by the Center. The LD moves to his right, and the RW moves back to check.

Purpose: Teach five-man (unit) reactions. The coach simply has the players align themselves in position. The players react to specific situations, such as the different possible positions of the puck, as the coach calls them out. A second method is to install the offensive unit and have short scrimmages (7 to 10 seconds). This will create various situations and enable the players to learn the different reactions under gamelike conditions.

Purpose: Teach the Center to shut down the middle. An offensive player (X1) attempts to pass to a forward (X3) cutting across the middle. The Center practices picking up the forward to prevent the pass from being completed.

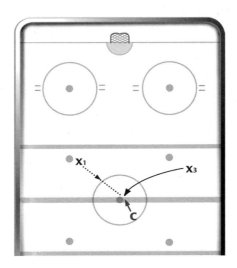

DEFENSIVE PLAY

The best teacher is repetition, day after day, throughout the season. It must be recognition and instant reaction.

John Wooden
They Call Me Coach

CHAPTER THREE

DEFENSIVE ZONE PLAY

GOOD DEFENSIVE ZONE PLAY REQUIRES THAT SIX PLAYERS ACCEPT THE RESPONSIBILITY and execute as a unit to prevent the opposition from scoring and to regain possession of the puck. Each individual must accept his place within the unit and execute his role.

The defensive team goes from attacking to defending in this zone, and the mood changes. More is at stake. The opposition is closer to scoring. There is less playfulness involved because the defensive team has less room for improvisation. Essentially, this zone calls for the basics. Fewer systems are available to a team when it is defending than when it is attacking the puck, and there is less room for errors: a mistake in the defensive zone is likely to result in a direct play on the net.

There are a number of key requirements that apply to all defensive systems:

1. Players must understand the system. Everyone must know each other's responsibilities as well as his own. If one player is beaten, the others must be able to adapt quickly.

2. When checking a player, always stay between the man and the net.

3. When playing the body, do it legally. Effective physical play is accomplished through proper positioning, not through holding, hooking, tripping, etc.

4. Accept the defensive responsibilities as an essential part of the game, equal to or even more important than the other parts.

Defensive play is fundamentally brief. The concepts are simple and direct. Yet the desire to defend is an intangible, and the coach needs to instill positive methods so that players will enjoy this part of the game. "This is what we're doing. This is what needs to be done. This will work."

The coach also needs to emphasize skills that are important to defensive zone play. Some examples are:

split vision—the ability to watch your man and/or zone and the play around the puck;

skating agility—the ability to move in short distances forward, backward and laterally;

body confidence—the ability to use balance, strength and power to defend in small areas.

Zone Defense

KEY POINTS

The Zone Defense is a conservative one. The defensive zone is divided into five sections, one for each player. The system calls for strict positional play, with limited freedom for players to be innovative. It asks the defensive players to outplay their offensive counterparts in all 1-on-1 situations. This system is used by all teams in certain situations. Young teams and those with limited skating ability find this system useful. It is a good system to teach individual players defensive coverage.

1. Zone Defense is a basic system that is easy to teach. It does not allow for much adaptation or innovation.

2. It stresses strict defensive coverage, with each player responsible for a given area of the ice surface.

3. It is a balanced defense, with the defensive zone divided into five zones.

4. It allows some overlapping of the zones.

5. The major weakness is that in a mobile game, it is easy for the offense to flood one zone with two or three players, creating a 2-on-1 or 3-on-1 situation.

Basic Alignment.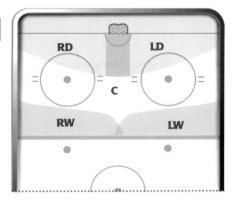
The defensive zone is divided into five zones. There is some overlapping of the zones. The wings cover the two points, the Center covers the slot area, and the defensemen cover from the front of the net to the corners.

The objective is to defend against the opposition by covering the entire 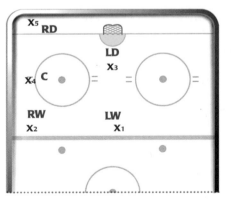 defensive zone. In a normal situation, one defensive player should be able to play the man or the puck in his zone. For example, if the opposition has the puck in the corner, the puck-side defenseman (RD) will play him. The other defenseman (LD) is in front of the net. The Center covers from the slot to the boards. The wings cover their respective points, maintaining a position between the puck and the point.

Combination Zone and Man-to-Man

KEY POINTS

This system, called the Combination, includes both conservative and aggressive approaches to defense. A sound understanding of the system's defensive principle is needed by all the players. The defensive zone is divided into five sections, each player responsible for one section; that's the conservative aspect. The players are then also given the freedom to adapt when one zone is flooded and its defensive player is outmanned. This allows the players to pressure the puck, the aggressive aspect. It is a good system for teaching the players to read and react. A team prerequisite is to have a good level of skating ability. Teams with physical players also find this system useful.

1. The Combination—Zone and Man-to-Man system is easy to teach, with straightforward objectives.

2. It stresses defending the different zones and taking into account the opposition's ability to flood the zones.

3. It encourages a measure of flexibility and innovation.

4. It depends on each player's ability to check successfully in 1-on-1 situations. It permits the players to leave their zones when another zone is flooded. This system does not want 2-on-1 situations to occur.

5. The major weakness is that discipline can be lost. Some players will have a tendency to run around, or "chase the puck," and leave their zones uncovered.

Basic Alignment. Each player has a zone for which he is responsible. **1** (See Zone Defense Diagram 1, page 53.) In addition to the zone, each player is responsible for one opponent. The wings cover the opposition's defensemen, the Center covers the opposition's center, and the defensemen cover the opposition's wings. The man-to-man coverage encourages more overlapping of the zones than in the strict Zone Defense.

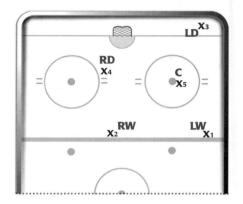

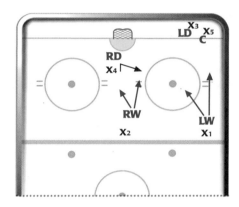

2 The objective is to prevent the opposition from creating any 2-on-1, 3-on-1 or 3-on-2 situations. When the opposition overloads one zone, a defensive player leaves his zone to cover his check. When this happens, the other players increase their zone areas. For example, if the Center goes to the corner to help the LD and to cover his check, the Center's zone (slot area) is vacated. The RW and the LW become responsible for the high slot, and the RD for the deep slot.

When the play moves into the defensive zone, the **3** wings normally go deep with their checks until the defensemen are able to assume their man-to-man responsibility. The Center normally moves to the slot area and covers the trailer, or if one of his wings has gone deep backchecking, the Center picks up the wing's responsibilities at the point.

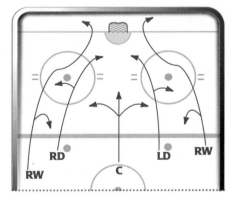

Box Plus One

KEY POINTS

The Box Plus One is an aggressive system of defense. It is a balanced system, with the two wings and defensemen forming a box. The box is similar to one for killing penalties (see page 206). The system's basic principle is to keep the offensive unit outside the box. The Center's role is to assist the other players, especially the defensemen. The Center prevents a defenseman from being caught in a 2-on-1 situation and allows the other players to be aggressive and attack the puck. The balance of the system permits the defensive team to attack the puck at every position. This advanced system is not suited to young teams or to those with poor skating ability.

1. The Box Plus One is an easy system to teach, with objectives that combine positional and man-to-man play.

2. It is similar to a penalty-killing situation, with the two defensemen and two wings forming a box.

3. The Center plays as a third defenseman, and he can also assist the wings.

4. It stresses shutting down the slot, often having two men in position to cover the slot.

5. It is flexible and can adapt to most offenses. It never asks a defensive player to check two men.

6. The opposition defenseman will often be forced to move to the slot area in an attempt to break up the box.

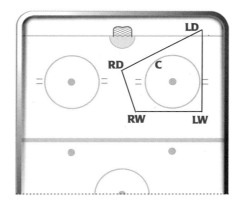

1 **Basic Alignment.** The defensive unit forms a box similar to a four-man penalty-killing formation. The puck-side defenseman (LD) plays the puck, and the other defenseman (RD) guards the front of the net. The puck-side wing (LW) covers his point closely, and the other wing (RW) is responsible for the high slot and the other point. The Center normally plays deep as a third defenseman.

The objective is to keep the **2** opposing team outside the box. The Center prevents the opposition from creating any 2-on-1 situations.

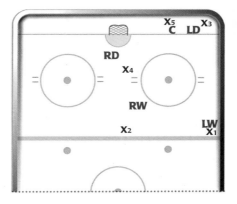

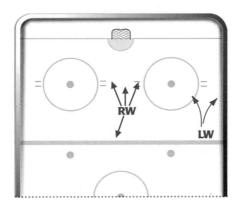

3 The wings have a multipurpose role. The puck-side wing (LW) plays his point tight. He can move in toward the face-off circle if the need arises; however, his main job is to cover the point. The off-side wing (RW) plays in the high slot. This allows the Center to be more aggressive and not to be as concerned with the slot. The puck has to go through the high slot to reach the point. The off-side wing is in a position to quickly cover the point.

The Center is crucial. His pattern **4** of movement resembles the spokes in a wheel. He never swings through the zone but moves back and forth in straight lines. He plays, primarily, as a third defenseman, and the three defensemen complement each other.

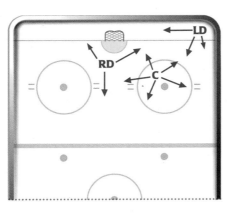

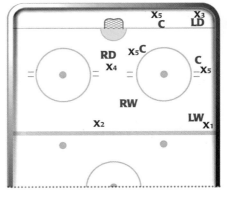

5 The Center must come back deep and concentrate on defense. If a second attacking forward is in the corner, the Center moves to the corner. If a second attacking forward goes to the net area, the Center must play the net area.

DRILLS

The following drills are examples that can be utilized to teach coverage in the defensive zone. Remember: Breakouts, clearing the zone with possession of the puck, are part of defensive zone play.

1 **Purpose:** Explain the defensive system, e.g., Zone. The coach goes through each position, describing the responsibilities of each player. The players should be familiar with each position, and the coach must *show* each player his turf. Defensemen: Responsible for area from far goal post to corner and out to the face-off dot. Center: Responsible for slot area from board to board. He has the largest area to cover. Wings: Responsible for area from blue line to top of face-off circle. The wings also have a man-to-man responsibility: they must attempt to limit the opposing defensemen's handling and shooting of the puck.

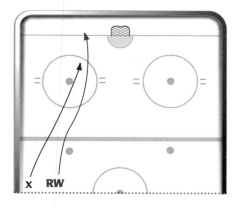

2 **Purpose:** Teach the wings proper backchecking technique. The drill is executed by having an offensive player (X) skate up the ice without the puck. The backchecking wing (RW) stays with X, keeping the following in mind:
1) He stays between X and the puck;
2) He stays within a stick's length of X to prevent him from breaking to the inside;
3) He must be aware of what is happening with the puck (repeatedly looks in direction of the puck);
4) He takes X to the goal post or to the corner;
5) He must exert total control over X, enabling the other players to concentrate on their jobs.

Purpose: Teach the defenseman **3** to play the man. The drill is executed by having an offensive player (X) attempt to skate out of the corner with the puck. The defenseman (RD) plays the man by keeping X to the outside and keeping himself between the puck and the net. The RD plays the man, thus separating X from the puck. An option is to add the Center to the drill. He moves in on the puck after the RD has taken control over X.

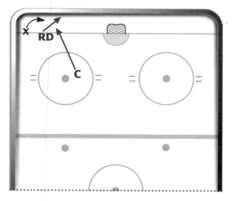

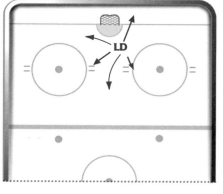

4 **Purpose:** Teach the defensemen proper position in front of the net. The off-side defenseman (LD) lines up on the far goal post. This permits him to view the entire puck-side area and not allow anyone to get behind him to the net. This positioning allows the LD to move to the opposition or the puck.

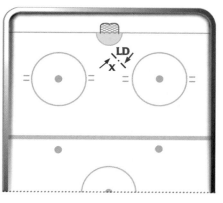

5 This drill should also have the LD practice picking up an offensive player (X) and keeping him from the front of the net. There is no action to this drill. Nevertheless, it is essential to show defensemen their position.

Purpose: Teach **6** the Center to defend the slot area. The Center stays with an offensive player (X5) in the slot area. A second offensive player (X4) is in the corner with the puck. A defenseman (RD) plays X4. X4 attempts to pass to X5, and the Center must keep X5 in check. An option is to have the Center move in on the puck if the RD takes X4 off it.

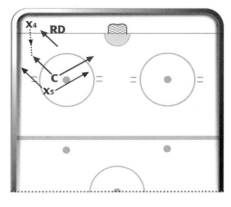

Purpose: Teach **8** defensive role of the puck-side wing. An offensive player (X3) is in the corner with the puck. X3 attempts to pass to the puck-side defenseman (X1). The puck-side wing (LW) checks X1 closely, preventing him from either receiving the puck or moving to the puck.

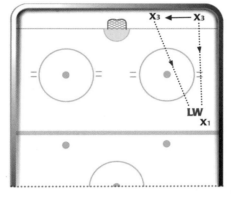

Purpose: **9** Teach the wings proper position while covering the points. The puck-side wing (LW) must cover his point man (X1) closely. He does this by staying within a stick's length and playing a little to X1's left. This prevents X1 from moving past the LW. The off-side wing (RW) plays his point (X2) more loosely (10 to 12 feet away). The RW plays to X2's right. This prevents quick access to the high slot for X2. Both wings must watch the puck and their respective points.

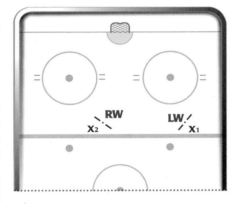

Purpose: Teach **11** defensive role of the off-side wing. An offensive player (X3) is in the corner with the puck. X3 attempts to pass to the off-side defenseman (X2). The off-side wing (RW), positioned between the puck and X2, attempts to intercept the puck. If the puck reaches the point, the RW prevents X2 from shooting or moving to the net.

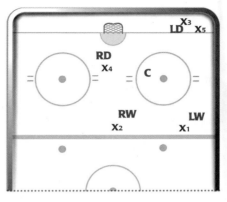

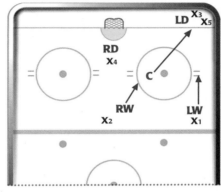

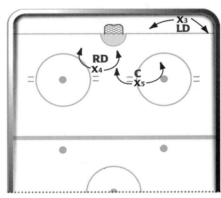

7 **Purpose:** Practice gamelike situations. This drill uses complete offensive and defensive units. The coach sets the players in any number of situations. The offense has the puck, and on the whistle, the defense adjusts to the offense in short (7-to-12-second) scrimmages. This drill familiarizes the players with their responsibilities for "Box Plus One." For example, in this setup, the LD is outmanned. On the whistle, the Center moves in to help the LD, and the RW moves in to the slot to help the RD cover the Center's slot area.

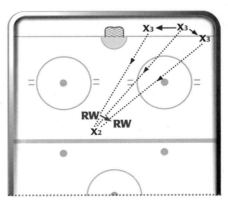

10 **Purpose:** Teach the interaction of the Center and the two defensemen. An offensive player (X3) has the puck in the corner. One defenseman (LD) covers X3. The RD and the Center set up according to the position of X4 and X5. Drill is essentially a 3-on-3. Defensive players must control their checks and gain possession of the puck.

SECTION
TWO

OFFENSIVE PLAY

On defense, you attack the puck. On offense, you attack *with* the puck. Offensive play is a blitzkrieg, an all-out attempt to overwhelm the other team with speed and strength and dazzling creativity. Much more room for innovation exists when your team goes on the offensive; in fact, quick reaction, unexpected adjustments and novelty are the essence of good offense. A goal scored is the ultimate unanticipated play, and the best systems of offense are the frameworks that generate the most opportunities for players to come up with something that no one is expecting.

Passing is crucial to success. Offense is all about moving the puck, and while there are times when one player carries the puck, for the most part, the puck should be advanced by passing. There isn't a player alive who can move at the speed of a brisk pass, and if a team is going to reap the rewards of effective offensive systems, then they must possess good passing skills. That means eliminating selfish play.

The players' individual strengths and weaknesses will be the main determinant of which offensive system the coach should choose. Fast-skating teams benefit from different systems than teams that emphasize size and strength. The former will likely use systems geared to open ice, while the latter are more apt to use those that direct play along the boards.

Readers will notice that this section of the book appears much more detailed than the material on defensive systems. That is because while defense is all about positioning and responding, offense is about decisive action—one thing leads to the next thing, which leads to the next. Despite the detail, coaches should keep in mind that these systems are, if anything, oversimplifications. As anyone who watches hockey knows, every moment contains infinite possibilities.

Coaches should also note that there is less and less direction possible (or desirable) as the offense moves into the opponents' end of the rink. Care and method are required to move the puck safely out of your own end, but from that point on, the possibilities for creativity and novelty should steadily increase.

OFFENSIVE PLAY

The players are out not only to make a good pass but to try to find a situation in which this pass will be most convenient and useful for their partners. And having made the pass, they once again strive to find themselves an opening to be on the receiving end this time.

Anatoli Tarasov
The Road to Olympus

CHAPTER FOUR

BREAKOUTS

B REAKOUT, OFFENSIVE PLAY IN YOUR OWN END, IS PERHAPS THE MOST CRUCIAL
systematic element of the offense. The attack begins when the offensive team
regains possession of the puck. Successful breakout plays do two things: First,
they allow the offense to clear its own zone; and second, they force the opposition to
play defense.

The systems for breakout plays are not complicated. They are deliberately kept
simple, because in your own end, it is execution that counts. Each player must know
what everyone else's responsibility is as well as his own. Breakout plays succeed when
everyone is in sync with everyone else. Breakouts call for teamwork.

Breakout plays should be worked on in every practice. Drills that utilize the entire ice
surface—for example, a 5-on-2 line rush—should be started as breakouts, and the coach
determines the success of the breakout plays by instilling the essential discipline into the
team.

Although there are not a lot of different systems for breakout plays, plenty of options
exist within that limited number. Teams should go slowly when learning breakouts. As
they progress, the options increase.

Coaches should keep in mind that breakouts especially benefit from moving the puck
quickly and that the best way to do that is to pass the puck. It is the ability of the team
to utilize the passing options that strengthens its attack. A sound attack begins with
sound breakout plays, because the entire attack is dependent on the offensive team
leaving its own end with confidence.

Positional Play

KEY POINTS

Virtually the first thing that young hockey players learn from coaches is where their positions are on the ice. The left wing is on the left, the right wing on the right, etc. Positional play at any level of experience is premised on the wings, the Center and the defensemen all staying in the lanes and the areas for which they are responsible. The Positional Play breakout is a conservative system. A forward is always in position to assume a defensive role if the puck is turned over. It is a balanced approach that utilizes all the players, and the offensive team can break out along either wing or up the middle. All teams must be familiar with this system; situations arise in every game that require it. The Positional Play breakout is especially important for young teams and for those with limited skating ability.

1. The Positional Play system is a conservative one with basic principles.

2. It stresses that one forward always be in position to move immediately to the defense if the puck is turned over.

3. It emphasizes high-percentage passes.

4. The defensemen "quarterback" the play.

5. It is a balanced system designed to use all three forwards, although it can be altered to emphasize a specific position.

6. Wings may cut across the middle to receive passes, but for the most part, everyone plays his lane.

DEFENSEMAN CARRIES THE PUCK

A defenseman carries the puck up the ice. He has a number of passing options.

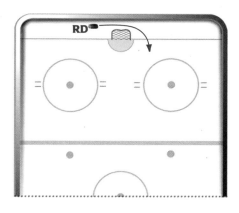

1 The defenseman (RD) has the puck and carries it behind the net. Without stopping, he moves up the ice with the puck.

The RD passes to the LW. **2**

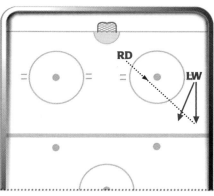

3 The RD passes to the Center.

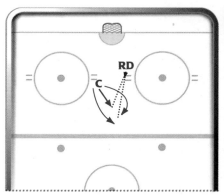

4 The RD passes to the RW, who is either moving toward or is in the neutral zone.

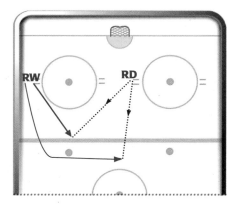

PLAYS

DEFENSEMAN TO WING (A)

**A defenseman swings behind the net with the
puck and passes to a wing on the boards.
The wing has a number of options.**

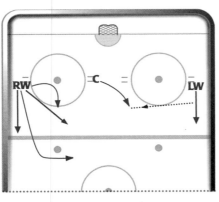

1 The defenseman (RD) has the puck and carries it behind the net. Without stopping, he passes to the LW. The LW can carry it up the ice.

The LW passes to the Center, who is moving toward him. The RW has a number of options: staying behind and following as a third forward, moving up his wing or moving across the ice. **2**

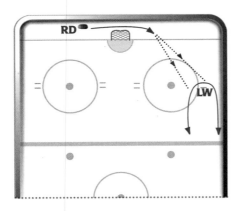

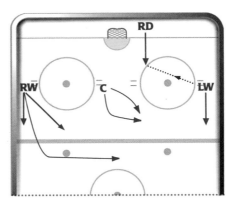

3 The LW passes back to the RD, who has continued up the ice after his initial pass. The RD can carry the puck or pass to any of the three forwards.

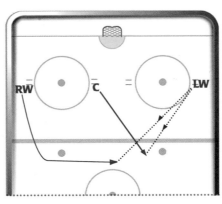

4 The LW can pass to the Center or to the RW in the neutral zone.

DEFENSEMAN TO WING (B)

A defenseman carries the puck behind the net and passes to a wing cutting across the face-off circle. The wing has a number of options.

The **1** defenseman (RD) has the puck and carries it behind the net. Stopping behind the net, he passes to the LW, who cuts across the face-off circle. The LW can carry the puck.

The LW **2** passes to the Center, who can move in a number of directions.

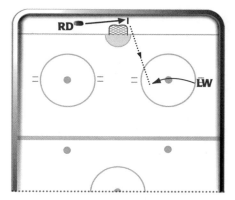

The LW **3** passes to the RW, who is either on his own wing or has moved to the middle.

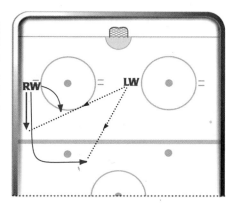

4 The LW passes to the LD, who can carry the puck or redirect it to any of the three forwards.

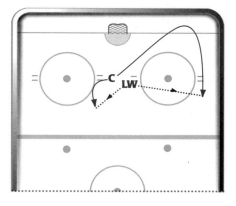

PLAYS

DEFENSEMAN TO WING (C)

A defenseman carries the puck behind the net and passes to a wing who has moved to the neutral zone. The wing has a number of options.

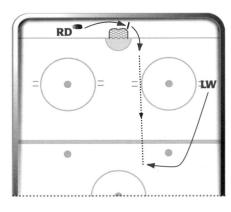

1 The defenseman (RD) has the puck and carries it behind the net. Stopping behind the net, he passes to the LW, who has moved out over the blue line and is cutting across the neutral zone.

The LW passes to the RW. **2**

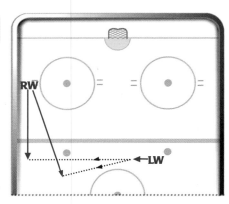

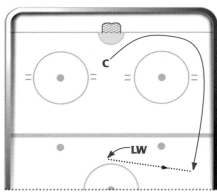

3 The LW passes to the Center, who has moved to the LW's wing.

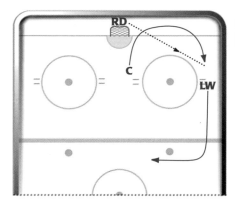

4 When the LW moves to the neutral zone, the Center swings over onto the left wing. This makes the Center a potential receiver of the RD's pass.

DEFENSEMAN TO WING (D)

A defenseman carries the puck behind the net and passes to a wing angling across inside the blue line. The wing has a number of options.

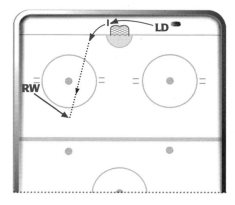

1 The defenseman (LD) has the puck and carries it behind the net. Stopping behind the net, the LD passes to the RW, who is angling across the zone toward the blue line.

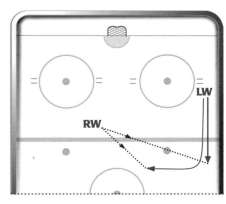

2 The RW passes to the LW, who is either moving toward the neutral zone or has already moved to that zone and is cutting across it toward the middle of the ice.

The RW **3** passes to the Center, who has moved in behind the RW's normal position.

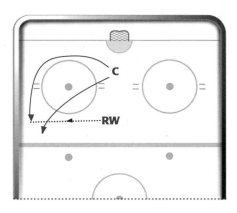

PLAYS

DEFENSEMAN TO CENTER (A)

A defenseman has the puck behind the net and passes to the Center, who has moved into the corner. The Center has a number of options.

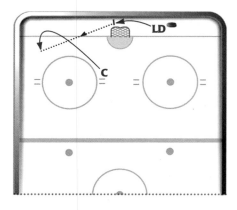

1 The defenseman (LD) has the puck and carries it behind the net. The Center swings into a corner. The LD passes to the Center.

When the Center swings into the corner, the wings have a number of options. **2**

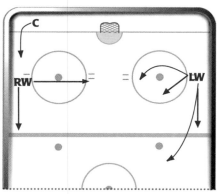

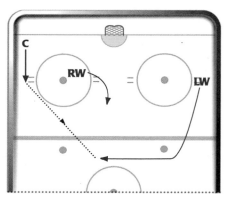

3 One example has the Center passing to the LW, who has moved to the neutral zone and is cutting across it. The RW moves up the middle.

When the Center moves up the ice **4** with the puck, the opposition has a tendency to move as a unit with him. This permits a defenseman (RD) to move up the ice behind the play. The RD is usually open, and the Center passes back to him. The RD has a number of options.

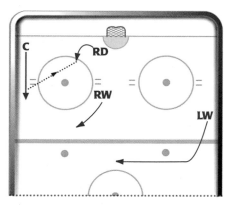

DEFENSEMAN TO CENTER (B)

A defenseman swings behind the net with the puck and passes to the Center in the slot. The Center has a number of options.

The defenseman (RD) has **1** the puck and carries it behind the net. Without stopping, he passes to the Center, who is skating across the slot. The Center can carry it up the ice.

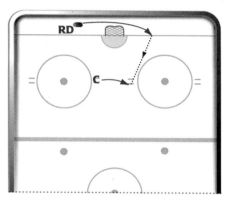

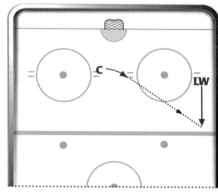

2 The Center passes to the LW, who is skating on his wing.

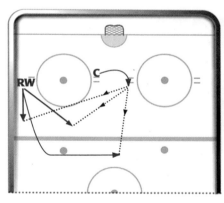

3 The Center passes to the RW, who is skating on his wing or coming across the ice either at an angle or by swinging out past the blue line.

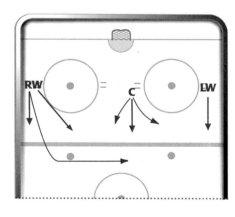

4 The forwards, working as a unit, each have specific avenues available.

PLAYS

DEFENSEMAN
TO DEFENSEMAN (A)

A defenseman has the puck behind the net and passes to the other defenseman, who has moved into the corner.

The defenseman (RD) has the puck and carries it behind the net. Stopping behind the net, the RD passes to the LD, who has swung into the corner.

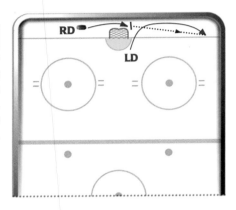

The LD passes to the Center, who has a number of options.

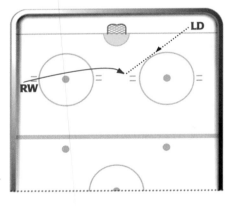

The LD passes to the RW, who has moved to the slot area after the LD vacated it.

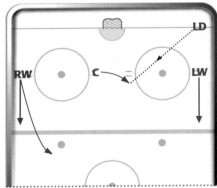

When the LD moves up along the boards, the RD often is open as the opposition also moves up the ice. The RD is able to move up the open slot area. The LD passes back to the RD.

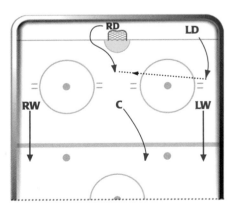

DEFENSEMAN TO DEFENSEMAN (B)

The defensemen pass the puck between themselves and then to the forwards.

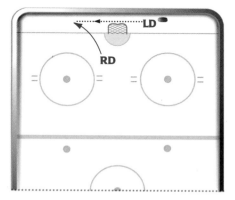

1 The defenseman (LD) has the puck deep behind the goal line. The RD moves to the other side behind the goal line. The LD passes to the RD.

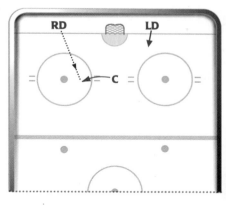

2 The RD passes to the Center, who has a number of options.

The RD passes to **3** the RW, who either carries the puck or passes to the Center.

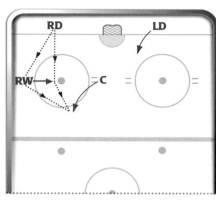

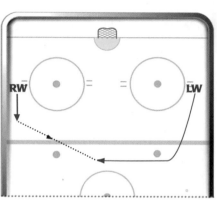

4 The RW passes to the LW, who is cutting across the neutral zone.

PLAYS

CENTER AND DEFENSEMAN
SWING INTO CORNER

A defenseman has the puck behind the net and passes to the Center or to the other defenseman in the corner.

The defenseman (RD) has the puck behind the net and has stopped. The Center and the LD swing into opposite corners.

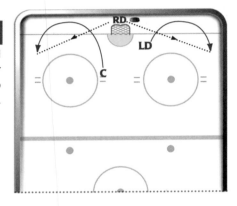

When the Center and the LD swing into the corners, the RW and the LW have a number of directions they can move.

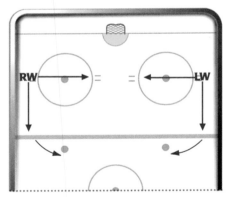

One possible play has the LD passing to the RW, who has cut across the slot. The RW has a number of options.

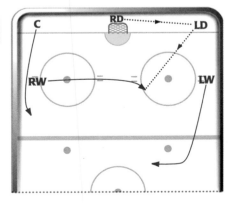

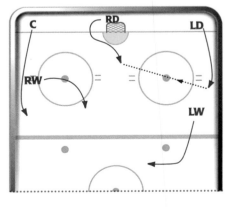

When the LD moves up the ice with the puck, the opposition has a tendency to move up the ice as a unit. The RD can move up the slot and is open for a pass back from the LD. The RD has a number of options.

CENTER GOES BEHIND THE NET (A)

The Center swings behind the net and picks up the puck. He has a number of options.

The defenseman (LD) has the **1** puck behind the net. The Center swings behind the net and picks up the puck.

The Center can carry the **2** puck up the ice, or he can pass to one of the wings, each of whom has a number of possible avenues.

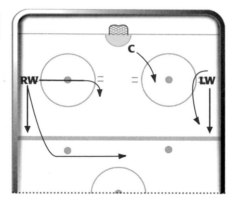

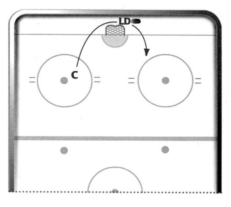

3 For example, the Center passes to the LW.

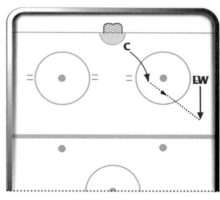

4 Another example, the Center passes to the RW.

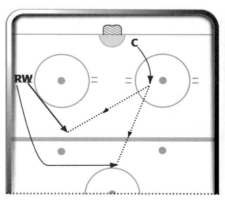

PLAYS

CENTER GOES BEHIND
THE NET (B)

The Center goes behind the net and does not pick up the puck.

The defenseman (LD) has the puck behind the net. The Center swings behind the net and into the corner. The Center leaves the puck with the LD, who then passes to the Center in the corner.

1

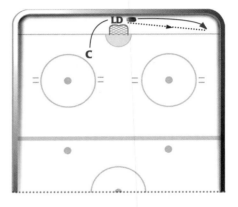

2 The Center can carry the puck up the ice. Or he can pass to one of the wings, each of whom has a number of possible avenues.

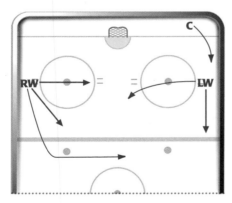

For example, the Center passes to the LW.

3

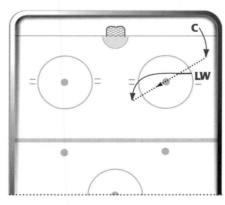

4 Another example, the Center passes to the RW.

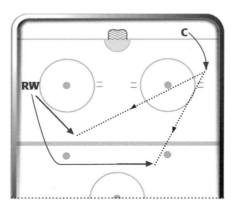

CENTER GOES BEHIND THE NET (C)

The Center swings behind the net and takes the puck.

The defenseman (RD) has the **1** puck behind the net. The Center swings behind the net and takes the puck.

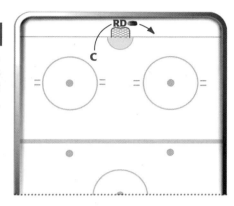

The Center **2** carries the puck up the ice. Often, the opposition's forechecker follows the Center. This vacates the front of the net. The Center passes back to one of the defensemen (LD), who has a number of options.

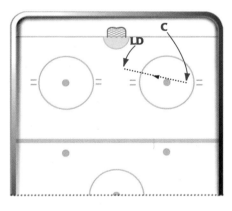

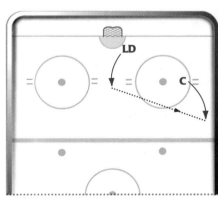

3 The LD makes a return pass to the Center.

The LD passes **4** to the LW.

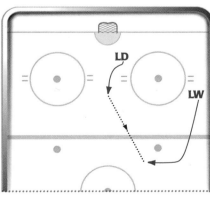

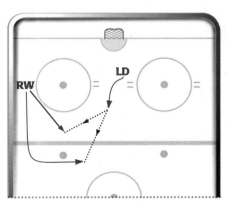

5 The LD passes to the RW.

Board Play

This is a conservative system with a limited number of options. The breakout passes are along the boards to the wings. No team should use this technique as its only system for breaking out, though it may be used as the predominant method of clearing the zone. This system best suits teams with big, strong wings who can dominate their check and count on winning the battle for the puck along the boards. It is important for the team to have forwards willing to be physical in these areas of combat. Small forwards, to play this system, must be adept at picking the puck up off the boards while moving. The wings are the *key* players in this system.

1. Board Play is a conservative style with objectives that are simple and direct.

2. The puck is directed toward the boards and away from the middle and the slot.

3. It is a balanced system, with both boards used equally.

4. The objective is to control the boards. This means controlling the puck and the opposition.

5. The wings are the key players in this system.

6. This style is called Board Play because the boards are used for *passing*.

7. Board Play is useful to defensemen who are under pressure.

BOARD PASS (A)

Defenseman passes to wing using the boards.

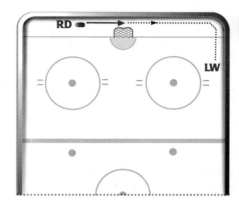

 The defenseman (RD) has the puck and passes to the LW using the boards.

The LW passes to the Center.

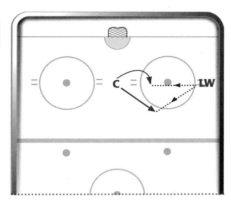

The LW passes to the RW.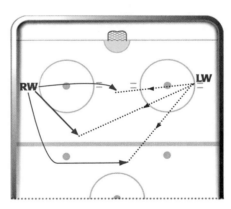

The LW passes back to the LD, who can carry the puck or pass again to one of the three forwards.

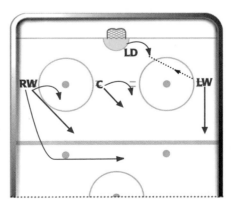

PLAYS

BOARD PASS (B)

A defenseman clears the puck from the net area using the boards to pass to a wing.

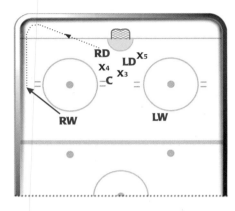

1 With the play in the net area, the RD gains control of the puck and passes it to the RW using the boards.

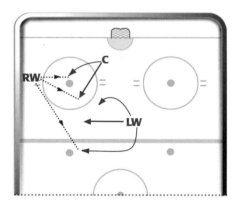

2 The Center and the LW move from their defensive positions to an area where they might receive a pass from the RW.

BOARD PASS— COUNTERDIRECTION

A defenseman has the puck and uses the boards to pass to a wing through the opposition's pursuit.

The defenseman (RD) **1** has the puck and is being pressured by X4 and X5.

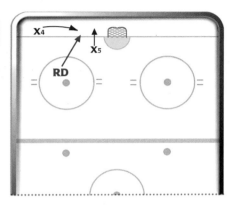

The RD passes to the RW **2** using the boards. This pass traps X4 and X5.

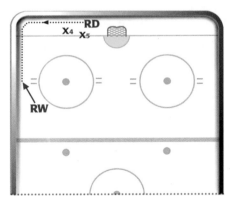

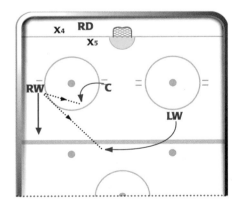

3 The RW can carry the puck or pass to the LW or the Center. The play should move up the ice quickly to take advantage of the trapped X4 and X5.

Free-Flowing System

KEY POINTS

Relying on good skating and expert passing, the Free-Flowing method permits great flexibility while breaking out. For it to work, players need to fully understand the system's principles: that the players and the puck are always moving to an open area and that everyone maintains precise puck control. The system does not abandon the concepts of Positional Play; rather, it is an extension of that system, utilizing a high level of skill to create more flexible breakout alternatives. The defensemen, usually "quarterbacks," often move the puck between themselves before passing to a forward. This is done to create open space. Coaches must watch closely that all players are comfortable with the added responsibility and freedom and that they remember their defensive roles.

1. The three forwards are always skating, and often the defenseman without the puck may be skating.

2. The system stresses well-developed passing skills.

3. The objective is to move the puck to an open area, with one or more forwards moving to the same area.

4. The defensemen are normally the "quarterbacks," although they may become part of the flow.

5. It is an unbalanced system, with the forwards flooding certain areas. The skating ability of the forwards minimizes the defensive shortcomings of the unbalanced structure.

6. It permits one forward to leave the zone before the puck. This opens the zone by forcing the opposition's defensemen off the blue line. It also creates quicker access to the neutral zone from the defensive zone.

7. This is all about anticipation, putting the puck where someone is going to be.

8. Everyone wants to play the Free-Flowing system.

COUNTERDIRECTION

The two defensemen pass between themselves to beat the quick pursuit of the opposition.

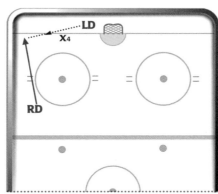

1 The LD has the puck and is being pressured by X4.

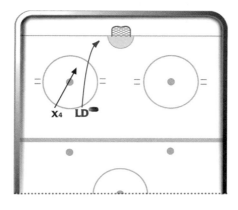

2 The LD makes a quick pass to the RD, who has moved back to give the LD an outlet.

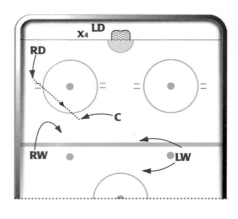

3 The three forwards move into areas where the RD can pass to them.

PLAYS

DEFENSEMAN
TO WING OR CENTER (A)

**A defenseman has the puck between the face-off circle
and the blue line. He passes to a forward up the ice.**

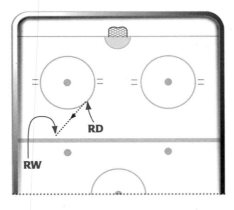

1 The RD has the puck and passes to the RW.

The RD has the puck and passes to the Center. **2**

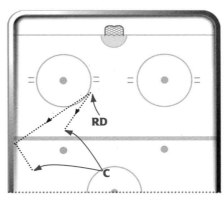

3 The RD has the puck and passes to the LW.

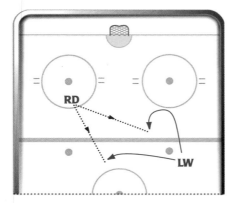

DEFENSEMAN TO WING OR CENTER (B)

A defenseman has the puck in the middle of the zone and passes to a forward up the ice.

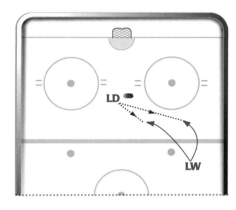

1 A defenseman (LD) has the puck in the middle of the defensive zone. The LD passes to the LW.

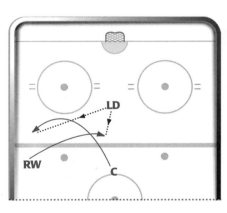

2 Two forwards (C and RW) crisscross near the blue line. The LD can pass to either.

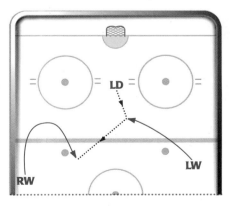

3 The initial pass to a forward should be followed with a quick second pass to another forward. For example, the LD passes to the LW, who quickly moves the puck to the RW.

PLAYS

FLOOD THE ZONE

A defenseman has the puck deep behind the goal line. The other defenseman and two forwards flood the zone, creating three possible pass routes.

A defenseman (RD) has the puck deep behind the goal line. Three players (RW, C and LD) move in front of the RD. The LW normally moves to the net to cover for the LD.

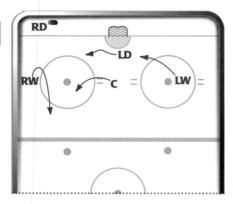

2 The RD can pass to any of the three players: the RW, the LD or the Center.

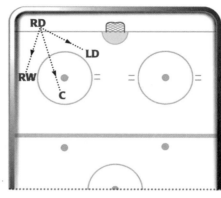

3 For example, the RD passes to the Center.

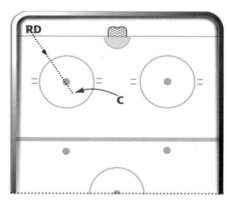

4 The Center moves the puck quickly to the RW, who is skating in the zone.

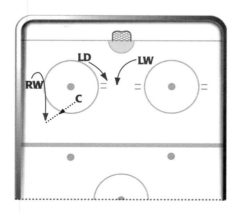

FREE-FLOWING (A)

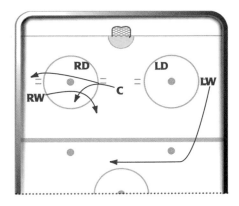

1 **Basic Pattern.** The LW moves to the neutral zone and skates across it. The RW and the Center swing back through the face-off circle and may or may not crisscross. The defensemen (LD and RD) have the option of passing to any open forward.

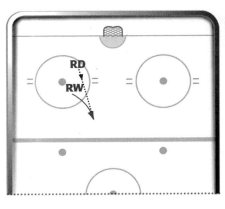

2 For example, the RD passes to the RW.

The RW **3** passes to either the Center or the LW.

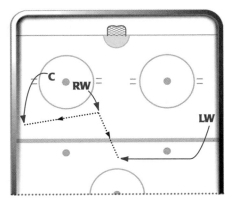

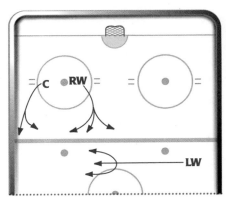

4 Whichever forward receives the pass from the defenseman has the option of passing to either of the other two forwards, who are skating into an open area.

87

PLAYS

FREE-FLOWING (B)

Basic Pattern. The LW either moves to the neutral zone and across it or cuts across the face-off circle. The RW and the Center swing, one high and the other low, through the face-off circle. The defensemen (LD and RD) have the option of passing to any open forward.

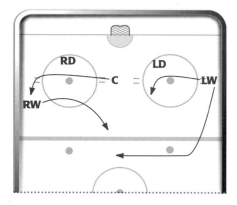

For example, the RD passes to the LW.

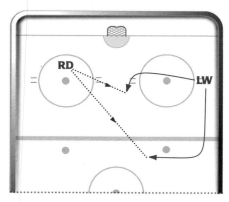

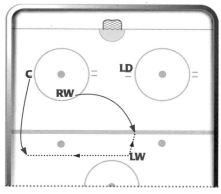

The LW passes to either the Center or the RW.

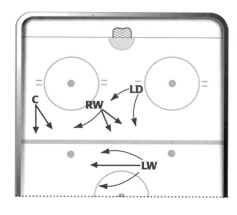

Whichever forward receives the pass from the defenseman has the option of passing to either of the other two forwards, who are skating into an open spot.

FREE-FLOWING (C)

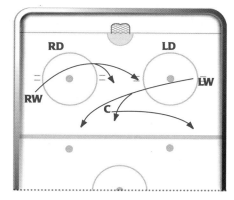

1 **Basic Pattern**. The Center swings to one side and can move to the neutral zone. The RW cuts deep across the zone and moves up the middle. The LW cuts across the middle of the zone toward the other side. The defensemen (LD and RD) have the option of passing to any open forward.

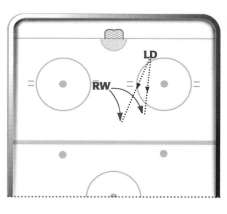

2 For example, the LD passes to the RW.

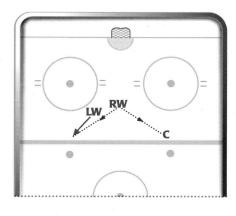

3 The RW passes to either the Center or the LW.

PLAYS

FREE-FLOWING (D)

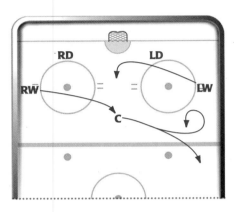

1 **Basic Pattern.** The LW swings toward the net and up the middle. The Center swings across the blue line and can go to the neutral zone or hook back into the zone. The RW cuts across the face-off circle and up the middle. The defensemen (LD and RD) have the option of passing to any open forward.

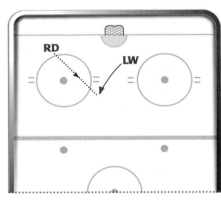

2 For example, the RD passes to the LW.

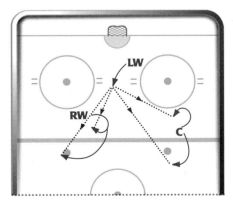

3 The LW passes to the Center or the RW.

FREE-FLOWING (E)

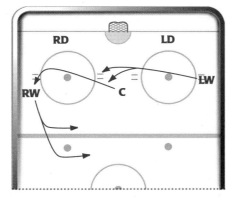

1 **Basic Pattern.** The RW moves toward the blue line, cutting across on either side of it. The LW swings deep and up the middle. The Center swings into the normal position of the RW. The defensemen (LD and RD) have the option of passing to any open forward.

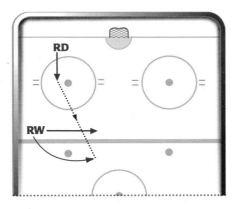

2 For example, the RD passes to the RW.

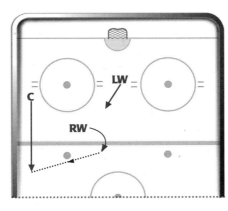

3 The RW passes to the Center. The LW follows up the play.

PLAYS

FREE-FLOWING (F)

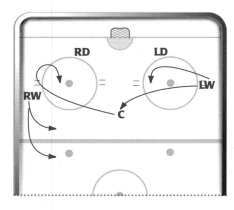

1 **Basic Pattern.** The RW moves toward the blue line, cutting across on either side of it. The Center swings toward the RW's side and curls in front of the RD. The LW either curls in front of the LD or cuts across the face-off circle and moves up the middle. The defensemen (LD and RD) have the option of passing to any open forward.

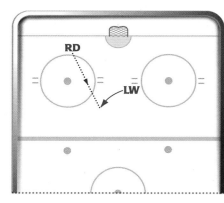

2 For example, the RD passes to the LW.

3 The LW passes to the RW. The Center follows up the play.

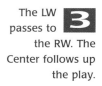

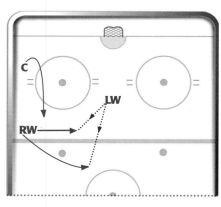

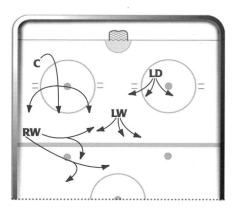

4 Whichever forward receives the pass from the defenseman has the option of passing to either of the other two forwards, who are skating into an open slot.

FREE-FLOWING (G)

Basic Pattern. The RW swings deep in front of the RD. The LW cuts across the middle of the face-off circle and up the middle. The Center moves up the middle toward the neutral zone and to either side. The defensemen (LD and RD) have the option of passing to any open forward.

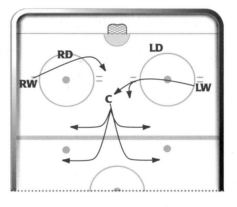

For example, the LD passes to the RW.

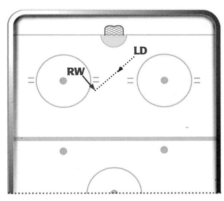

The RW passes to either the Center or the LW.

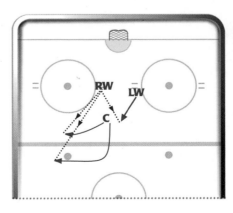

PLAYS

FREE-FLOWING (H)

Basic Pattern. The LW swings deep in front of the LD and up the middle. The RW hooks into the face-off circle. The Center moves toward the LW's side and back across the blue line. The defensemen (LD and RD) have the option of passing to any open forward.

1

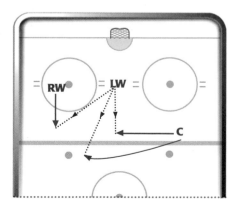

2 For example, the RD passes to the LW.

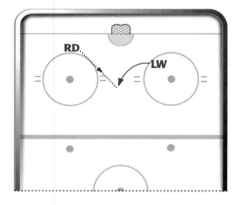

The LW passes to either the RW or the Center.

3

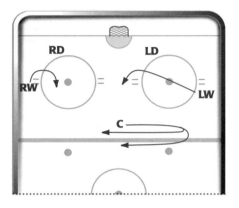

FREE-FLOWING (I)

Basic Pattern. The RW and the Center crisscross near the top of the face-off circle. The LD moves up the middle. The LW swings back into the LD's position and can follow up on the play. The RD can pass to the LW, the Center or the LD.

1

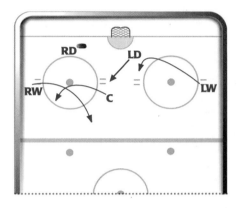

For example, the RD passes to the LD.

2

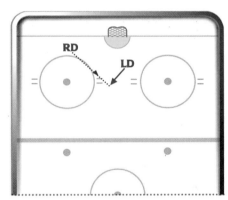

3 The LD passes to either the Center or the RW.

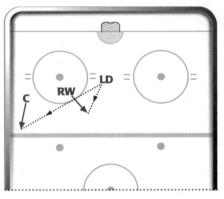

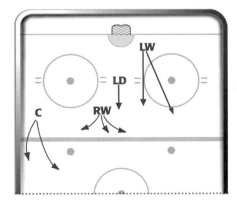

4 Whichever player (LD, RW or C) receives the pass from the RD has the option of passing to the other players, who are skating into an open slot.

95

PLAYS

FREE-FLOWING (J)

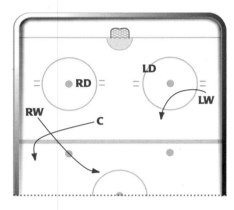

1 **Basic Pattern.** The LW hooks high in the face-off circle. The RW and the Center crisscross high near the blue line. The defensemen (LD and RD) can pass to any open forward.

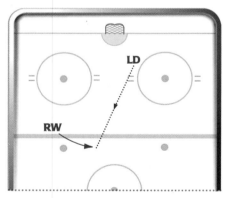

2 For example, the LD passes to the RW.

The RW passes to the Center, and the LW follows up on the play. **3**

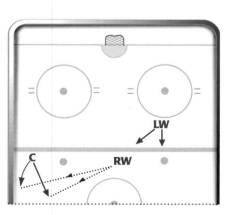

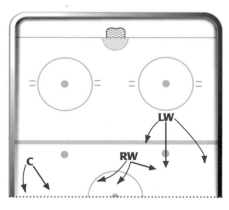

4 Whichever forward receives the pass from the defenseman has the option of passing to either of the other two forwards, who are skating into an open slot.

FREE-FLOWING (K)

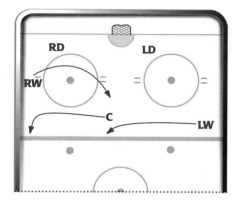

1 **Basic Pattern.** The RW swings across the face-off circle and up the middle. The Center and the LW move to the right, high toward the blue line. The defensemen (LD and RD) can pass to any open forward.

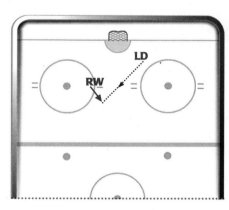

2 For example, the LD passes to the RW.

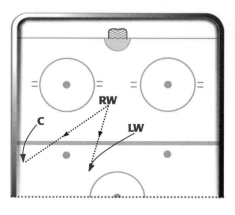

3 The RW passes to either the LW or the Center.

PLAYS

FREE-FLOWING (L)

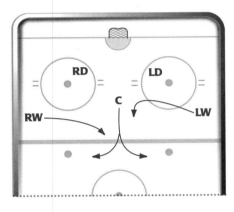

1 **Basic Pattern.** The Center moves to the neutral zone and cuts either way. The RW and the LW cut into the middle. The defensemen (LD and RD) can pass to any open forward.

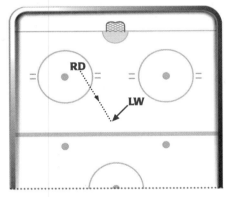

2 For example, the RD passes to the LW.

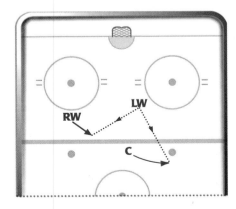

3 The LW passes to either the Center or the RW.

FREE-FLOWING (M)

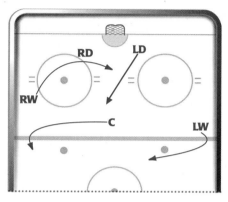

1 **Basic Pattern.** The Center cuts across the zone inside the blue line. The LW cuts across the neutral zone outside the blue line. The LD moves up the middle. The RW swings deep and moves into the LD's normal position. The RD can pass to the Center, the LW or the LD.

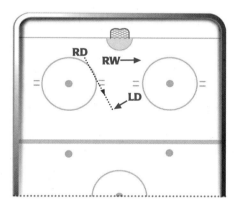

2 For example, the RD passes to the LD.

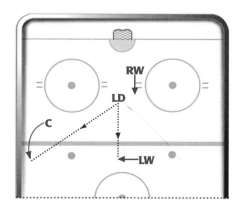

3 The LD passes to either the Center or the LW. The RW can move up the zone.

DRILLS

A number of drills can be used to teach the different breakout plays. Three examples are shown using a step-by-step approach: 1. Defenseman to Center, 2. a Board Play, and 3. a Free-Flowing Play. A good method of teaching breakout plays through drills is to do the following:

1. Demonstrate the proper positioning and the various options of the play;

2. Have the players walk through the play (half speed);

3. Have the team execute the play (three-quarters progressing to full speed);

4. Increase the difficulty of the play by inserting the opposition's players.

Many of the steps can be made into drills for 1-on-1s, 2-on-1s, 3-on-2s, etc.

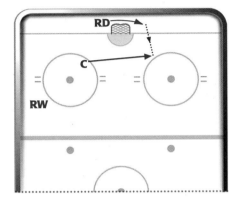

1 **Defenseman to Center Demonstration**
The defenseman (RD) swings behind the net and passes to the Center, who is coming across the slot.

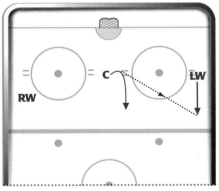

2 The Center can pass to the LW or carry the puck.

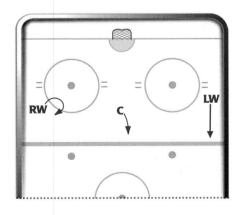

3 The three forwards break out of the zone, with the RW coming from behind. (This can develop into a 3-on-1 or a 3-on-2 drill.)

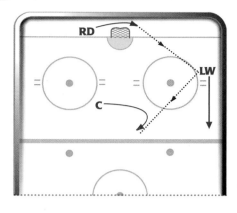

4 The RD swings behind the net and passes to the LW, who is either stationary on the boards or moving up the ice. The LW carries the puck up the ice. (This can develop into a 1-on-1 drill.) Or the LW can pass to the Center, who is moving up the middle. (This can develop into a 2-on-1 drill.)

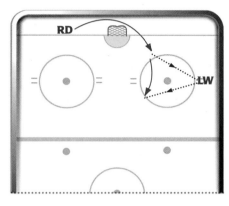

5 The RD swings behind the net and passes to the LW. The RD continues to move up the ice and receives a return pass (give and go) from the LW. (This can develop into a 1-on-1 or a 2-on-1 drill.)

6 The RW is inserted into Steps 4 and 5. The off-side wing (RW) moves a couple of strides toward the slot. This prevents him from getting ahead of the play and teaches him his defensive role. (This can develop into a 3-on-1 or a 3-on-2 drill.)

7 **Walkthrough and Execution** Practice the above options 5-on-0. Be sure to cover each option.

8 **Execution With Difficulty** Insert one forechecker (X5) to forecheck the puck. The LD should screen out X5 as part of the drill.

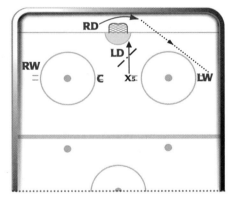

9 Insert more forecheckers. It is this step that begins to simulate gamelike conditions.

10 The forechecking unit works systematically. The offensive unit needs to be able to clear the zone against a full forechecking unit in practice to gain the confidence to do so in a game.

11 Have short scrimmages (10 to 15 seconds) by starting at different points in the breakout play.

DRILLS

**Board Play
Demonstration
and Walkthrough**

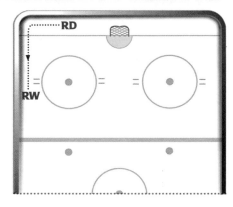

1 The defenseman (RD) passes the puck along the boards to the near wing (RW).

The RW carries the puck out of **2**ᴀ the zone. (This can develop into a 1-on-1 drill.)

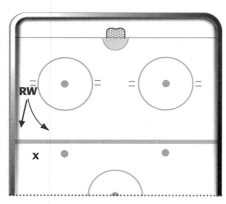

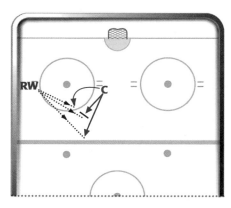

2ʙ The RW passes to the Center, who is swinging toward the boards, moving up the ice or setting a pick (to work a give and go with the RW). (This can develop into a 2-on-1 drill.)

The three forwards move out **3** of the defensive zone as a unit. The LW moves toward the slot area (for defensive purposes) and comes from behind the play. (This can develop into a 3-on-1 or a 3-on-2 drill.)

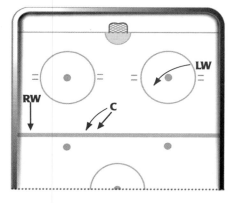

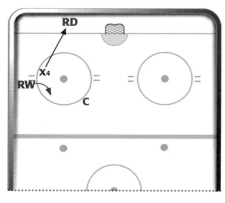

4 Insert one forechecker (X4), who forechecks the puck and the RD. Either the RW or the Center should interfere with X4 to give the RD more time.

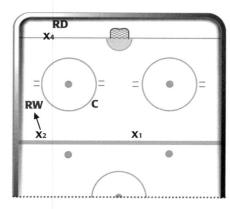

5 Insert a second forechecker (X2), who pinches along the boards on the RW. The RW must control the boards. If the RW is not able to control the puck, he must immediately check X2. (This can develop into a 1-on-1 or a 2-on-1 drill, with the opposition's other defenseman, X1, being the defenseman.)

7 Have short scrimmages (10 to 15 seconds) by starting at different points in the breakout play.

6 Insert the other members of the forechecking unit. It is this step that begins to simulate gamelike conditions. The forechecking unit works systematically. The offensive unit needs to be able to clear the zone against a full forechecking unit in practice to gain the confidence to do so in a game.

Free-Flowing Play Demonstration and Walkthrough

1 The defenseman (RD) passes the puck to the RW. The RW practices the different routes available to him. (This can develop into a 1-on-1 drill.)

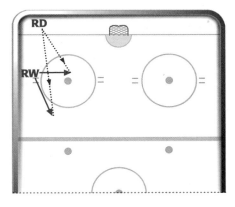

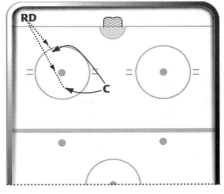

2 The defenseman (RD) passes the puck to the Center. The Center practices the different routes available to him. (This can develop into a 1-on-1 drill.)

3 The defenseman (RD) passes the puck to the LW. The LW practices the different routes available to him. (This can develop into a 1-on-1 drill.)

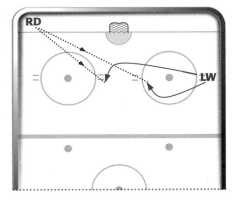

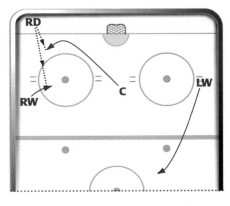

4 The defenseman (RD) passes the puck to either the Center or the RW. The LW simultaneously moves to the neutral zone. (This can develop into a 2-on-1, a 3-on-1 or a 3-on-2 drill.)

5 The three forwards break out of the defensive zone, with the RD making the outlet pass. (This can develop into a 3-on-1 or a 3-on-2 drill.)

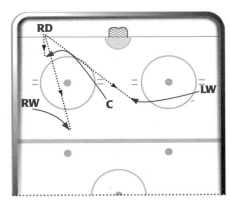

6 The coach goes through the different patterns. The forwards, in particular, must be familiar with each option. The defensive responsibilities must be clearly understood.

7 Insert one forechecker (X3) to forecheck the puck. The above steps can be executed with the one forechecker.

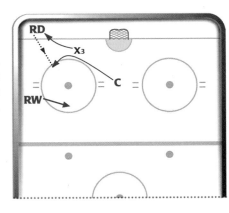

8 Insert more forecheckers. It is this step that begins to simulate gamelike conditions.

10 Have short scrimmages (10 to 15 seconds) by starting at different points in the breakout plays.

9 The forechecking unit works systematically. The offensive unit needs to be able to clear the zone against a full forechecking unit in practice to gain the confidence to do so in a game.

OFFENSIVE PLAY

Although not every coach can win consistently with talent, no coach can win without it.

John Wooden
They Call Me Coach

CHAPTER FIVE

NEUTRAL ZONE OFFENSE

H ISTORICALLY, COACHES HAVE OFTEN OVERLOOKED NEUTRAL ZONE OFFENSIVE play. It was as if the offense just passed through the center-ice no-man's-land on its way to the scoring zone at the other end of the rink. In reality, effective neutral zone play translates into a better attack, and most often, the team that wins the battle in the neutral zone wins the game. An offensive squad that can make its way decisively across the neutral zone crosses the opponents' blue line with initiative and tempo on its side; the defenders, on the other hand, are set back on their heels, scrambling to reorganize.

The objective of neutral zone offense is to generate the attack. The better the execution, the quicker and stronger the attack. Offensive play in this zone is either the counterattack, which follows regaining possession of the puck in the center-ice area, or the attack link between the breakout and the offensive melée in the opponents' end.

The systems of attack that a team employs should therefore be consistent from zone to zone, and the offensive play and individual responsibilities must be similar for the players whether the play is a counterattack or the attack link. It is crucial that the players have a thorough understanding of the principles of their system and that they be taught to use their time in the neutral zone effectively and not just skate for the other end of the rink.

As always, the coach must keep in mind his personnel's abilities when selecting a system for the neutral zone, and he should give careful consideration to this underappreciated aspect of the game when he is making plans and deciding on offensive strategies.

This chapter has two parts. Part One presents three basic systems of neutral zone play: Positional Play, Forwards Crisscross and Regroup/Free Movement. This section suggests systems that provide the guiding principles to neutral zone offense. Part Two presents a number of specific plays and suggests ways to generate the attack as it moves over the blue line into the offensive zone.

Positional Play

KEY POINTS

The Positional Play system in the neutral zone is a conservative one that complements the Positional Play breakout system. It is a balanced system that utilizes all the players. The basic traditional positions have the wings in the outside lanes, the defensemen in the inner lanes and the Center in the middle. A forward is always in position to assume a defensive role if the puck is turned over. This system calls for short, direct, high-percentage passes. All teams, regardless of their ability, must be familiar with this system because situations requiring it arise during every game that every team plays. It also is a foundation for all systems of play in the neutral zone. This system is especially beneficial for teams with size and/or poor skating ability.

1. The Positional Play system is a conservative style of offense. It is easy to teach, since everyone simply plays his position.

2. It stresses playing and controlling the neutral zone's lanes.

3. It emphasizes a basic style of play: head-man passes, short and direct passes, 2-on-1 situations, etc.

4. This system emphasizes control of the boards in the neutral zone.

5. "Dumping the puck" is permitted but only as a predetermined play. One forward must be in position to get to the puck first or quick enough to pressure the opposition if possession of the puck is lost.

6. The defensemen are conservative. They primarily move the puck to the forwards. When they move up, they do so to fill a lane.

7. Positional Play enforces the discipline needed to win the neutral zone.

This system allows some interchanging **1** of the lanes. The wings and the defensemen are allowed to move between two lanes, while the Center is allowed to play all five.

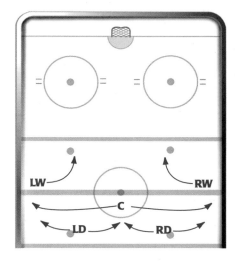

2 The normal procedure has the wings staying in their lanes. If a wing (LW) moves to another lane, three things can happen:
1) The Center moves to the wing's lane;
2) A defenseman (LD) moves to the wing's lane;
3) The LW and the Center create a 2-on-1 situation as they double up on one of the two opposing defensemen.

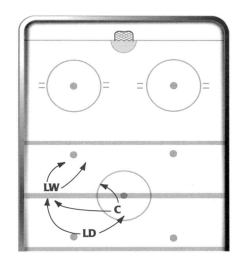

If a wing (LW) is ahead of the **3A** play, the Center has to head-man the puck to the LW, who either stays in his lane or moves over a lane. The Center reacts to the LW's play. The LD can move up to fill a lane or remain at his position.

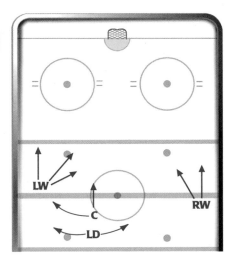

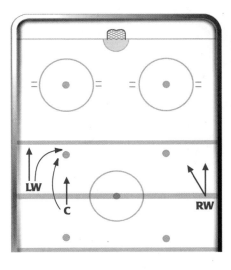

3B If the LW is skating but covered, the Center can clear the red line and dump the puck if he thinks the LW can get to it first. The LW can also cut across the blue line and set a pick to clear a lane for the Center.

If the wings are coming from behind the play, the Center has a number of options:

He holds the puck and sets **4**ₐ up a 2-on-1 situation against a defenseman (X1). The wings must break; i.e., head straight for the blue line.

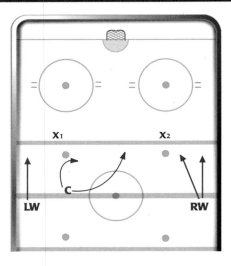

He swings wide and **4**ᵦ carries the puck deep along the boards with the wing (LW) following. This creates a 2-on-1 situation on a defenseman (X1) in a vertical alignment.

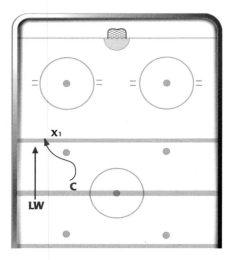

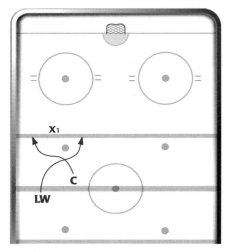

4c He cuts to the boards, and the wing (LW) cuts to the middle. This creates a different 2-on-1 situation on a defenseman (X1).

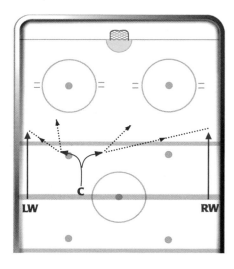

4ᴅ He slows down or stops close to the blue line, permitting the wings to break in for a pass or to be in position to gain possession of the puck if it is dumped in.

If the defensemen **5**A have the puck, they should never keep it and force the forwards to stop skating. Their responsibility is to move the puck and keep the forwards skating. The forwards can move up the ice or across into other lanes.

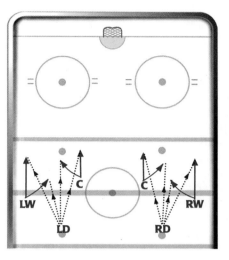

The defensemen can work **5**B a give and go. The defenseman (LD) passes to a wing (LW) and moves up to receive a return pass, creating a 2-on-1 situation on the defenseman (X1) for the LD and the Center.

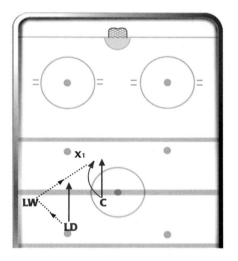

If the forwards are **5**C covered but skating, the defenseman (LD) can dump the puck and two forwards (LW and C) will converge on it.

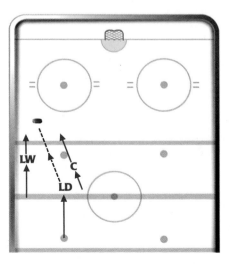

DRILLS

To teach this positional system, set plays should be practiced. This is not done to regiment the players but rather to teach proper execution. As the number of plays that are mastered increases, the team will become aware of the options and the situations in which they can be used. The plays can be practiced in any number of situations: three forwards, two forwards, two forwards and a defenseman, or all five players against anywhere from no opposition to all five defending players. The plays can end on a play on goal or simply by clearing the neutral zone with the puck. A few plays are shown for examples.

The Center has the puck and is ahead of the LW. He attempts **1** A to open the outside lane by forcing the defenseman (X1) to turn with his swing to the middle. If X1 turns, the Center will pass to the LW. If X1 does not turn, the Center will carry the puck.

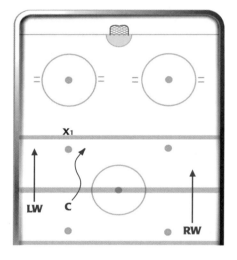

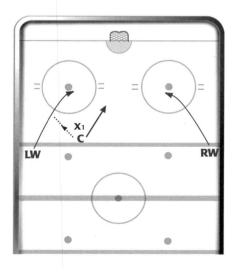

1 B If the LW receives the puck, the off-side wing (RW) breaks for the net. The LW has the option of shooting, passing to the RW or continuing to the net, with the Center moving to the slot for a return pass.

A wing (LW) is ahead of the Center, who has the puck. The Center passes to the LW and then swings to the boards. The LW has a number of options: passing to the Center on the outside; passing to the off-side wing (RW), who is breaking; or carrying the puck himself. His reaction will be partly determined by the defenseman's (X1) actions. The options for the net are the same as in Play 1.

2

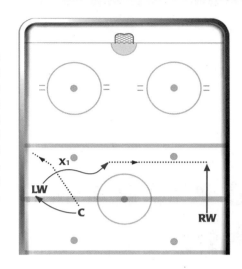

One defenseman (RD) has the puck, with the forward ahead of the play. The other defenseman (LD) moves up his lane and receives a pass. The LD moves the puck quickly to an open forward. His options are numerous, but accurate passing is essential.

3

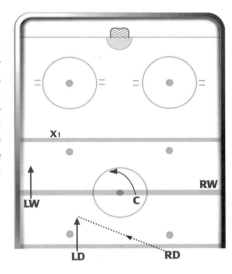

4 For instance, a quick pass to the LW may create a 2-on-1 situation for the LW and the Center on X1. The options for attacking the net are similar to Plays 1 and 2.

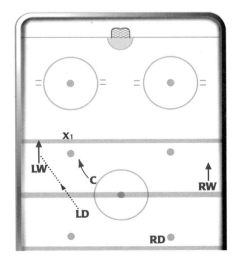

Forwards Crisscross

KEY POINTS

The Forwards Crisscross system combines conservatism with free movement. The conservative aspect of this system is that one forward, usually a wing, remains in a stable position with defensive responsibilities if the puck is turned over. The extra freedom is a result of the two remaining forwards being encouraged to move laterally and to flood specific areas. For example, the RW stays in his lane while the Center and the LW crisscross. This system can be used by any team once it has mastered the Positional Play system. The players must have competent skating and puck-handling skills if this system is to be effective.

1. The Forwards Crisscross system combines conservatism with limited free movement. The "limits" make it easy to teach.

2. It emphasizes quick skating and crisp passing.

3. One forward has a static or nonmoving role. He becomes the safety valve for the defensemen and often relays the puck to the two skating forwards.

4. Dumping the puck should be used only as a last resort. If it is done, the puck should be directed to an area on which the skating forwards can quickly converge.

5. The defensemen are conservative. They usually move the puck to the forwards. When they move up, it is done to fill a lane.

The off-side wing (RW) goes 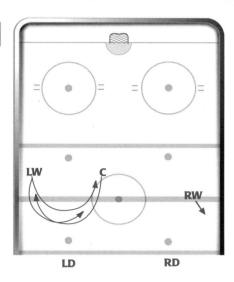 to the boards. The puck-side wing (LW) and the Center crisscross. The crisscrossing can be done in any number of patterns (Diagrams 1a-1b). The LD will normally move the puck to the skating forwards. He may pass to the RD, who then passes to the skating forwards. The different patterns allow the forwards to find open spaces.

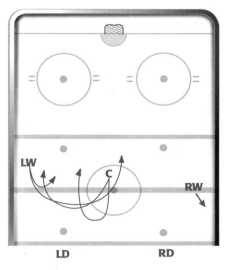

The off-side wing (RW) plays a 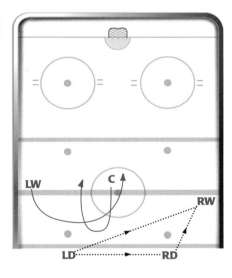 key role. He provides stability because he is always on the boards. He is the safety valve and is often in position to relay the puck from the defensemen to the skating forwards.

A variation of this 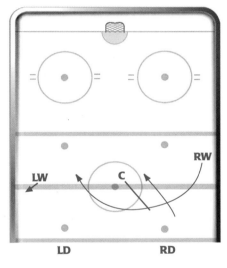 neutral zone offense is to have the puck-side wing (LW) go to the boards while the off-side wing (RW) and the Center crisscross.

This variation can be used 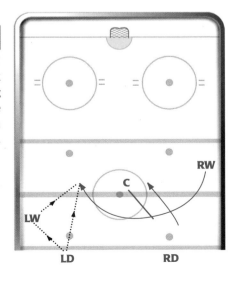 when the opposition has a particular weak side. The crisscrossing forwards should move toward the LD for a quick pass.

If the LD makes a 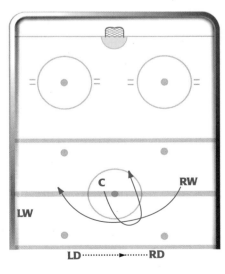 quick pass to the RD, then the LW becomes the off-side wing and the system reverts to the mirror image of that shown in Diagrams 1 and 2.

DRILLS

To teach the neutral zone play for this system, specific steps should be taken leading up to practicing set plays. The free movement means that the offensive unit must be familiar with the different patterns. In addition, the conservative play of the off-side wing means that the remaining two skating forwards must be well synchronized and react quickly to each other.

The movement of the puck to the off-side wing (RW) is important. **1** Proper positioning of the wing is critical. Practice moving the puck to both the off-side and puck-side wings. Passes direct from the LD as well as from defense to defense (LD to RD) should be practiced.

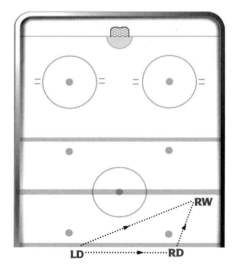

2 The different patterns of the criss-crossing forwards should be practiced. No pucks should be used initially. The off-side wing can be added. (This can be a skating drill.)

Pucks are added to Step 2, with a defenseman (LD) passing to the crisscrossing forwards. Other options include having the LD pass to the RD, who in turn passes to the forwards; and adding a third forward, who comes from behind the play. (This can develop into drills such as 2-on-1 and 3-on-2.) (Steps 3a-3c)

3A

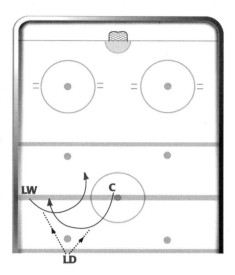

3B

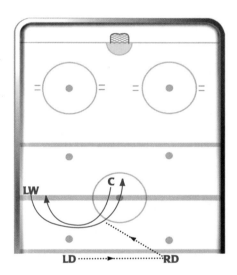

3C

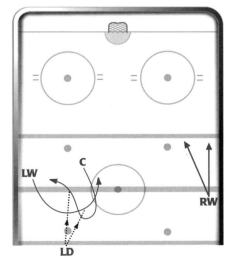

4 The offensive unit practices the different situations. At this stage, set plays can be developed. The end result can be a play on goal or simply clearing the neutral zone.

5 The defensive unit is inserted to provide opposition. The normal procedure is to begin with the defensemen and progress to the forwards.

Regroup Free Movement

KEY POINTS

The Regroup/Free Movement system abandons the traditional conservative aspects of neutral zone play. The forwards are always skating, looking for or creating openings. Puck control is essential for this system. Players regroup in order to control the puck until an opening to the offensive zone is found, then the forwards attack that opening. The free-movement aspect permits the forwards maneuverability in the zone. It is an aggressive system in the sense that the forwards remain in constant motion, ready for quick movement toward any area. It is important for the coach to emphasize that the freewheeling forwards still have defensive responsibilities in the event of a turnover. This system can be employed only by teams with a high level of skill development.

1. The Regroup/Free Movement system calls for constant motion from the forwards.

2. The constant motion makes it a difficult system to teach in a short period of time.

3. Skillful puck handling is vital.

4. The objective is to control the puck until the forwards are able to create an opening into the offensive zone.

5. The defensemen quarterback the play but are also permitted to move into the openings.

6. Advanced development of the technical skills—skating, passing and stickhandling—is crucial for this system to be successful.

The three forwards keep in constant motion. This movement creates an almost infinite number of patterns. Practice different possibilities. Diagrams 1a-1d illustrate four possible patterns. (This can be a skating drill.)

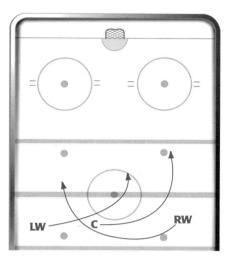

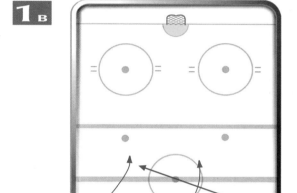

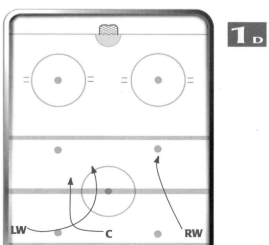

117

Diagrams 1e-1h illustrate four of the more intricate patterns available to teams with greater skating ability. (These can be skating drills.)

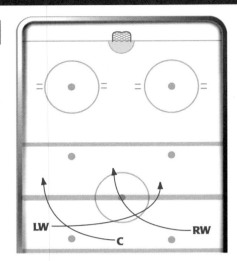

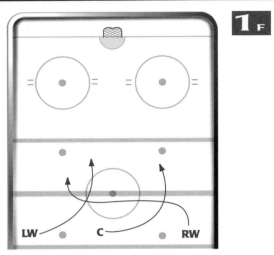

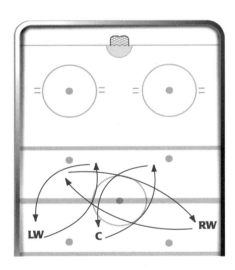

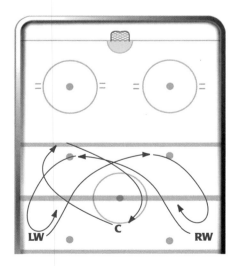

The coach must limit the 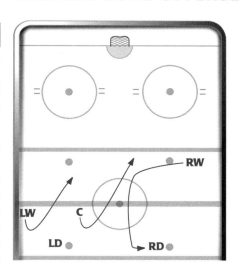 number of patterns with specific guidelines. For example, if the forward farthest from the puck (RW) has the defensive role, the other two forwards have unlimited freedom to create an opening. The RW can become a decoy. For example, the RW can cut across the red line and turn back toward the defensemen. The RW stays in position defensively. If the RW has been successful in clearing the defensive for- 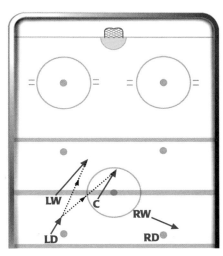 ward from the area, the Center and the LW will move to the area, and the defenseman with the puck (LD) will know that that is the potential opening and be prepared to move the puck in that direction.

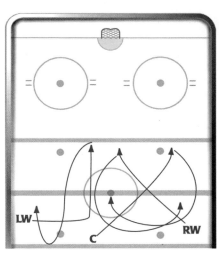

If an opening is not created on the initial rush, the forwards regroup, move back toward the defensemen and make another rush. Skating ability and puck control make this tactic possible. Often the forwards turn back with the puck and pass back to the defensemen to initiate the regrouping.

Regrouping can be a tactical move. The opposition may have a tendency to break down or get out of position during regrouping. The forwards will look for a player who gets out of position and attack that area. For example, the opposition's left defenseman (X2) may move up the ice too quickly when the offensive unit regroups. The RW and the Center will regroup, while the LW will move toward the area X2 may vacate. The two defensemen will anticipate this. The LD passes to the RD, who will pass to the LW if he is open.

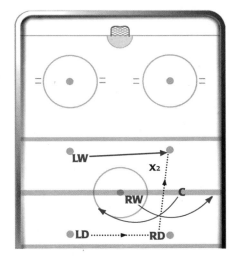

119

DRILLS

To teach the neutral zone play for this system, specific steps should be taken to lead up to specific set plays. Free movement means that the offensive unit must be familiar with the different patterns and become accustomed to anticipating each other's moves correctly.

The different patterns of the skating forwards should be practiced. No pucks should be used at the start. (This can be a simple skating drill.) **1**

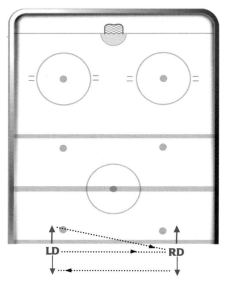

2 The defensemen must be adept at passing and controlling the puck. Have the two defensemen practice passing between each other. They must be able to move with confidence in small areas with the puck and while passing.

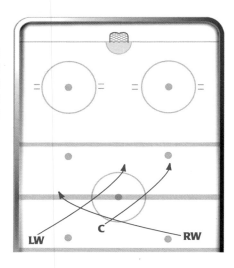

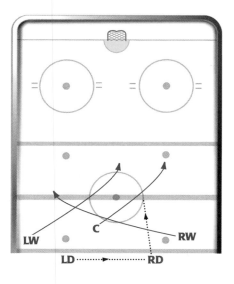

3 The above two steps are combined. The defensemen pass the puck to the forwards. (This can develop into drills such as 3-on-1 and 3-on-2.)

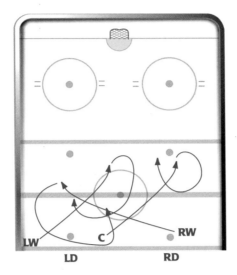

4 The forwards stay in the neutral zone to practice regrouping. This teaches puck control as well as the attack from the regrouping.

The offensive unit moves into the offensive zone on a 3-0 or 5-0.

5

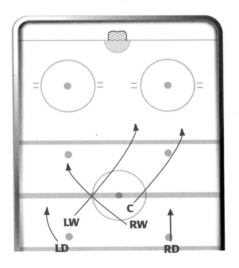

The defensive unit is inserted to provide the opposition. The normal procedure is to begin with the defensemen and progress to the five-man unit.

6

121

Neutral Zone Attack

KEY POINTS

This section presents plays for entering the offensive zone. These are not systems but more specific suggestions for the patterns of players as they move into the opponents' end of the rink. Players need to know this kind of information so that they will discipline their play as they attack across the far blue line. These plays are good practice drills. The coach should teach several of these plays, but not all of them. Hockey is not like basketball, where the coach is able to call out the plays as the team moves up the court. Include these plays in 2-on-1 and 3-on-2 drills. Whether the drill starts at the red line, the far blue line or the far end, the players need to have an idea of what is going to happen as they move up the ice. Practicing plays that emphasize entering the offensive zone accomplishes this.

1. Players must have a general idea of what they are going to do while moving up the ice.

2. The team should be familiar with a limited number of plays, not a large number.

3. The plays must permit a flexible framework that encourages innovation.

4. Entering the offensive zone as a coordinated unit intensifies the attack.

DUMP THE PUCK (A)

The Center has control of the puck and shoots it deep into a corner. The wing on that side is skating toward the corner to regain control of the puck.

The Center has the puck, clears the red line and shoots it deep into the RW's corner. The RW is skating toward the corner.

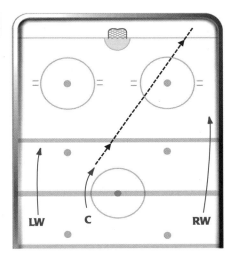

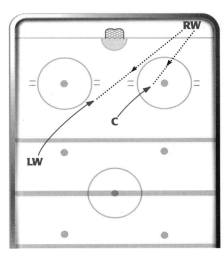

The RW has the puck deep in the corner. The Center moves toward the right side and is in a position to follow or back up the RW. The LW moves to the slot. The RW has the option of passing to either forward.

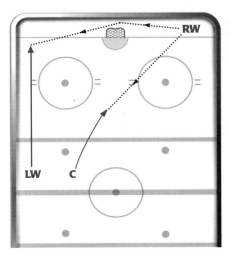

The RW has the puck deep in the corner. The LW goes deep on his wing. The Center moves to the slot. The RW has the option of passing to either forward.

PLAYS

DUMP THE PUCK (B)

A wing has the puck and shoots it deep to the opposite corner. The other wing is skating toward the corner to regain control of the puck.

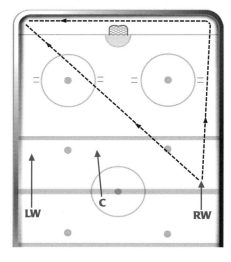

1 The RW has control of the puck, clears the red line and shoots it deep into the LW's corner. This is done either diagonally or around the boards. The LW is skating toward the corner.

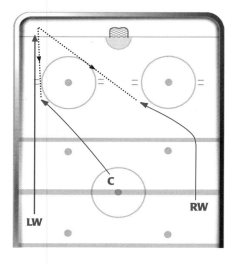

2 The LW has the puck deep in the corner. The Center moves to the left side and is in a position to follow or back up the LW. The RW moves to the slot. The LW has the option of passing to either forward.

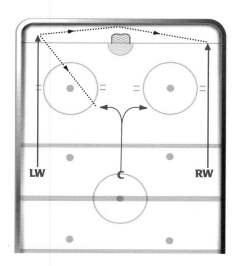

3 The LW has the puck deep in the corner. The RW goes deep on his wing. The Center moves to the slot. The LW has the option of passing to either forward.

CENTER CONTROLS THE PUCK (A)

The Center has control of the puck and head-mans it to a wing.

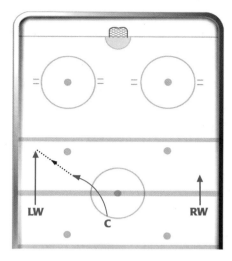

1 The Center has control of the puck in the neutral zone and passes to the LW. The LW is ahead of the puck and forces the Center into head-manning the puck.

2 The LW has the puck entering the offensive zone. The Center moves to the left and follows the LW. The RW moves to the slot. The LW has the option of passing to either forward.

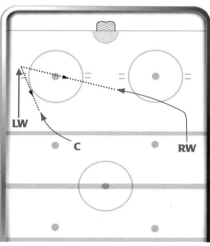

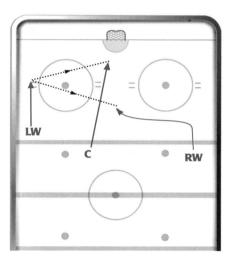

3 The LW has the puck entering the offensive zone. The Center moves to the net. The RW moves across to the slot. The LW has the option of passing to either forward.

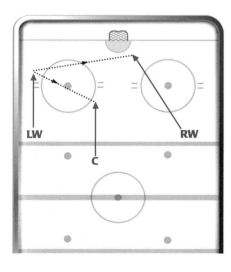

4 The LW has the puck entering the offensive zone. The Center moves to the slot. The RW goes directly to the net (the goal post on his side). The LW has the option of passing to either forward.

PLAYS

CENTER CONTROLS
THE PUCK (B)

**The Center has control of the puck
and passes to a wing.**

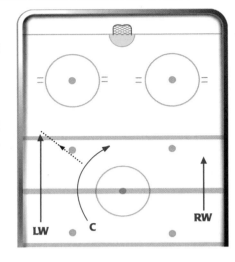

1 The Center has control of the puck and cuts first toward the left wing and then back toward the middle. The Center passes to the LW

2 The Center makes this move in an effort to get the opposition's defenseman (X1) to move with him toward the middle. If X1 moves toward the middle, the outside lane opens for the LW.

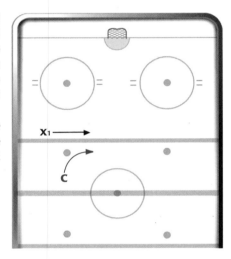

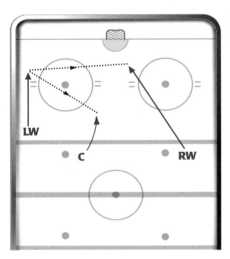

3 The LW has the puck entering the offensive zone. The Center moves to the slot. The RW goes directly to the net (the goal post on his side). The LW has the option of passing to either forward .

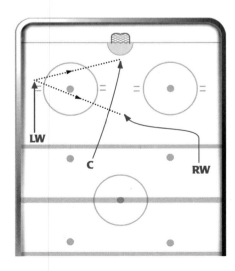

4 The LW has the puck entering the offensive zone. The Center moves to the net. The RW moves across to the slot. The LW has the option of passing to either forward.

The Center has control of the puck. He moves to the left side and ahead of the LW. The Center crosses the blue line, carries the puck along the boards and either back passes or makes a drop pass to the LW.

1

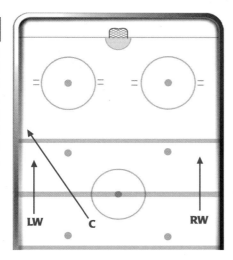

CENTER CONTROLS THE PUCK (C)

The Center has the puck and carries it across the blue line.

The Center carries the puck along the boards. This is done to make the opposition's defenseman (X1) turn and move with him. This opens up the LW for the pass.

2

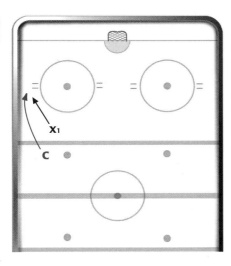

3 The LW has the puck near the blue line. The Center continues deep along the boards. The RW goes directly to the net (the goal post on his side). The LW has the option of passing to either forward.

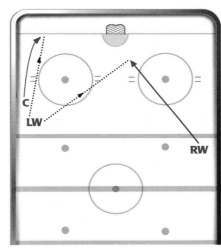

4 The LW has the puck near the blue line. The Center moves to the net area. The RW moves across to the slot. The LW has the option of passing to either forward.

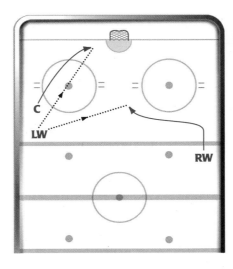

PLAYS

CENTER CONTROLS THE PUCK (D)

The Center has the puck, crisscrosses with a wing in the neutral zone and makes a drop pass.

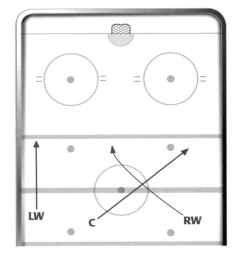

1 The Center and the RW crisscross in the neutral zone. The Center drops the puck to the RW.

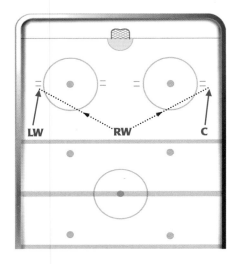

2 The RW has the puck entering the offensive zone. The Center moves along the right boards, and the LW along the left boards. The RW has the option of passing to either forward.

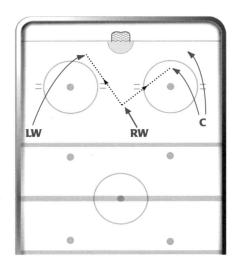

3 The RW has the puck entering the offensive zone. The LW moves to the net area. The Center moves deep along the boards. Note: Virtually the same play can begin with a crisscross and drop pass to the RW that takes place just inside the blue line.

CENTER CONTROLS THE PUCK (E)

The Center has control of the puck and lead passes to the wide wing in the offensive zone.

The Center has the puck and passes to the wide wing (RW) near the blue line.

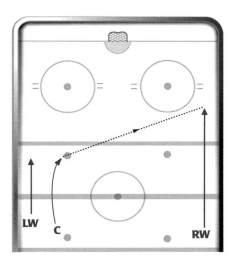

The RW carries the puck in the offensive zone. The LW goes to the net area. The Center moves to the slot. The RW has the option of passing to either forward.

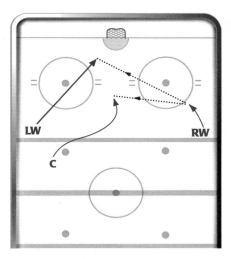

The RW carries the puck in the offensive zone. The Center goes to the net area. The LW cuts across the slot. The RW has the option of passing to either forward.

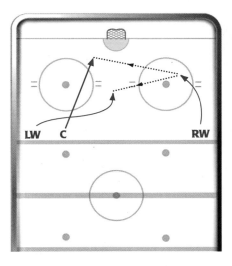

PLAYS

CENTER CONTROLS THE PUCK (F)

The Center has control of the puck and passes to the wide wing in the neutral zone.

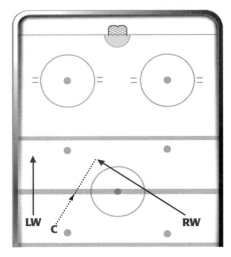

1 The Center has control of the puck in the neutral zone. The wide wing (RW) breaks to the middle and in front of the Center, forcing the Center to head-man the puck to him.

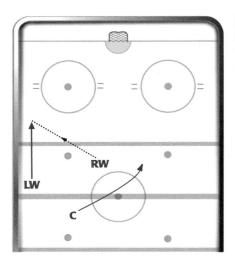

2 The RW passes to the LW at the blue line.

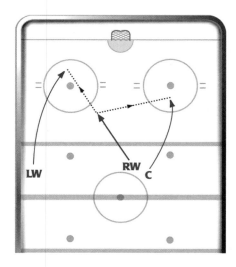

3 The RW carries the puck into the offensive zone. Both the Center and the LW move deep into the zone. The RW has the option of passing to either forward.

The Center carries the **1** puck into the offensive zone. He goes deep to one side (left side) to make a play.

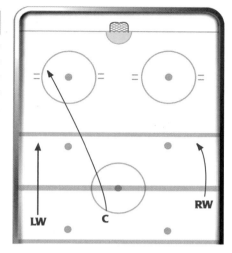

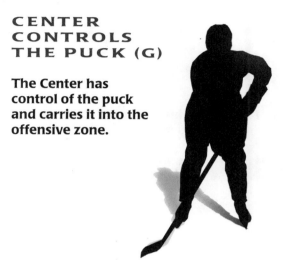

CENTER CONTROLS THE PUCK (G)

The Center has control of the puck and carries it into the offensive zone.

The RW moves to the slot **2** area. The LW follows behind the Center. The Center has the option of passing to either forward.

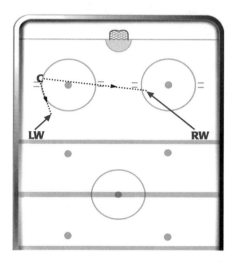

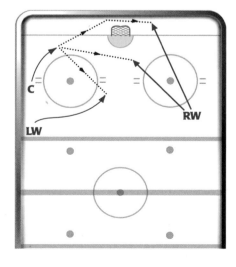

3 The RW moves deep, either to the net area or behind the goal line. The LW moves to the slot area. The Center has the option of passing to either forward.

PLAYS

CENTER CONTROLS
THE PUCK (H)

**The Center has control of the puck and
carries it into the offensive zone.**

The Center
carries the **1**
puck into the
offensive zone
and stops inside
the blue line.

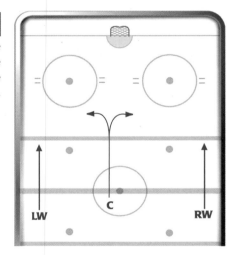

2 The Center
passes
quickly to the wing
(LW) while the other
wing (RW) moves to
the net area. The LW
passes to the RW.

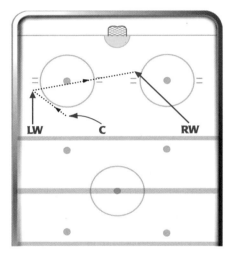

3 Both wings
(LW and
RW) move deep
toward the net.
The Center has the
option of passing
to either wing.

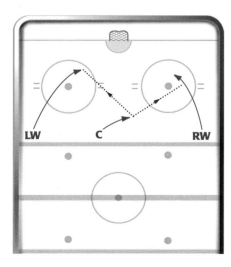

CENTER CONTROLS THE PUCK (I)

The Center has control of the puck. One wing screens or picks a defenseman, and an offensive defenseman fills the lane.

The Center has control of the puck in the neutral zone. The RW moves across the red line, and the RD fills in the lane behind the RW.

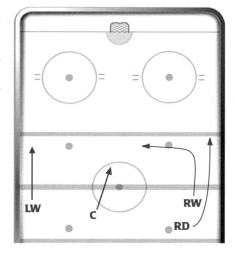

The RW moves across the blue line in an attempt to draw the opposition's defenseman (X2) with him, and the RW is able to screen or pick X2 out of the play.

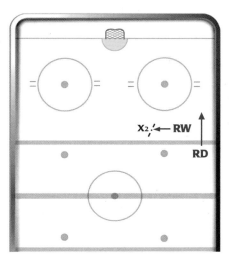

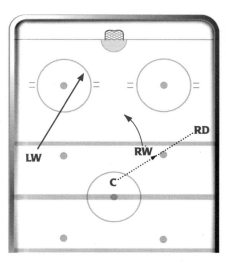

The Center passes to the RD, who has moved to the blue line. The LW breaks for the net area. Either the Center or the RW moves to the slot. The other covers for the RD on the blue line.

PLAYS

WING CONTROLS THE PUCK

A wing has control of the puck and cuts toward the middle, near the blue line.

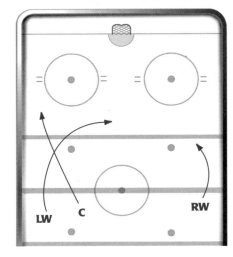

1 The LW has control of the puck and cuts to the middle, near the blue line. The Center cuts to the left side, behind the LW. The RW stays along the boards. The LW can make a drop pass to the Center.

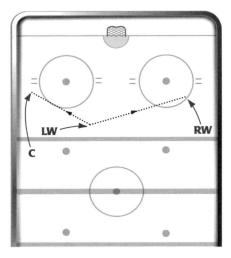

2 The LW has the puck near the blue line. The RW and the Center move along the boards. The LW has the option of passing to either forward.

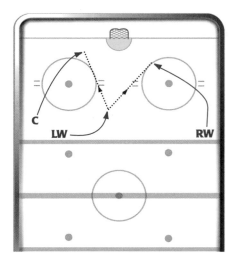

3 The LW carries the puck into the slot area. The Center and the RW move deep into the slot area. The LW has the option of passing to either forward.

The Center has control of the puck and moves to the left side. Both wings stay on their wings. The LD moves into the area vacated by the Center.

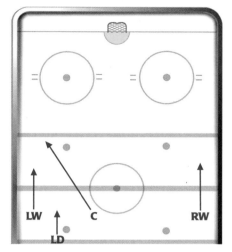

DEFENSEMAN MOVES UP THE PLAY

A defenseman moves up on the play in the neutral zone, filling a lane.

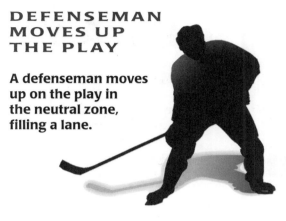

The LW stays back, while the LD moves into the offensive play.

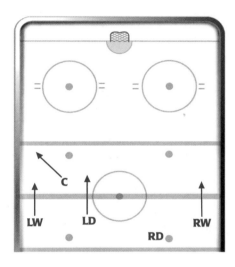

The Center carries the puck into the offensive zone. The RW cuts across into the high slot. The LD moves through the slot to the net area. The Center has the option of passing to either the LD or the RW.

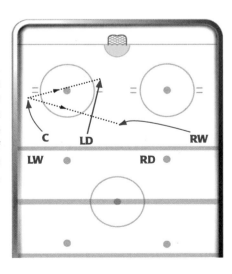

The Center carries the puck into the offensive zone. The RW moves to the net area. The LD goes to the high slot. The Center has the option of passing to either the RW or the LD.

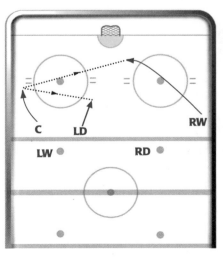

PLAYS

CENTER STAYS BACK

**The Center stays back and a
defenseman moves up.**

The Center
swings back
through the middle.
The LW moves to his
right in the direction
of the Center's normal
lane. The LD moves
into the LW's normal
lane on the boards.
The RW stays on
his side.

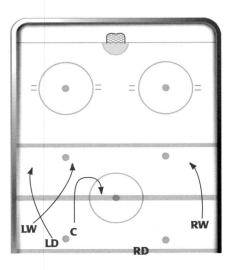

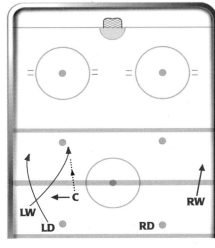

The Center has
the puck,
passes to the LW and
moves to cover the
LD's position. The LD
moves up the left side.

The LW carries
the puck into
the offensive zone.
The LD moves along
the left boards. The
RW moves to the net.
The LW has the option
of passing to either
the RW or the LD.

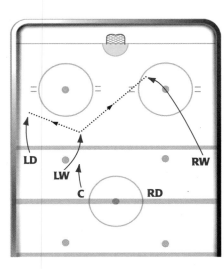

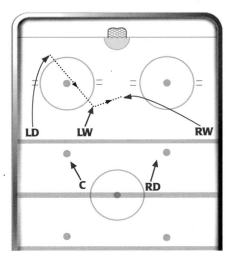

The LW
carries the
puck into the offen-
sive zone. The LD
moves from the left
side toward the net.
The RW cuts across
into the high slot. The
LW has the option of
passing to either the
LD or the RW.

One possible shift has the Center and the RW moving to the left. The LW swings in behind the Center and the RW.

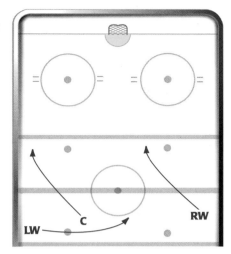

FORWARD SHIFT

The three forwards shift within the neutral zone. This is done to force the opposition's defensemen to switch coverage.

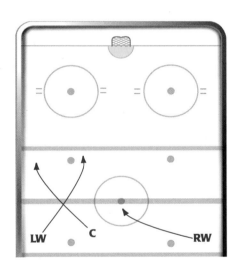

2 A second shift has the LW and the Center switching lanes. The RW moves to his left and can either move directly to the offense or follow the LW and the Center.

Using the second example, the LW carries the puck into the offensive zone. The Center moves down the left side, and the RW goes to the net area. The LW has the option of passing to either the Center or the RW.

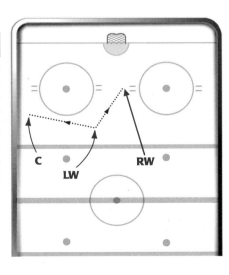

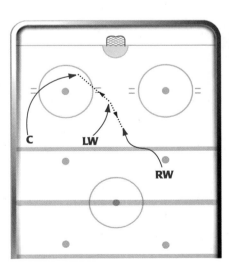

4 The LW carries the puck into the offensive zone. The Center moves from the left side toward the net. The RW follows the LW into the high slot. The LW has the option of either passing to the Center or making a drop-pass or back-pass to the RW.

PLAYS

FORWARDS REGROUP (A)

The three forwards regroup in the neutral zone. This is done after the initial attempt to move into the offensive zone is stopped.

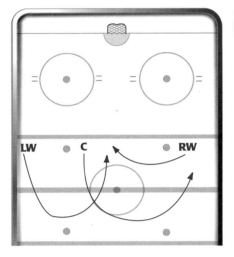

1 The skating patterns of the three forwards while they are regrouping in the neutral zone.

2 The LW has the puck and passes back to the LD. The three forwards skate their patterns.

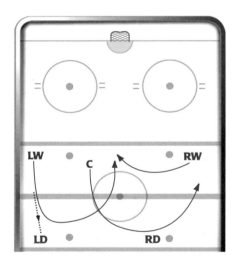

3 There are a number of possible passing plays. The RD and the LD can pass to the forwards any time during their regrouping patterns.

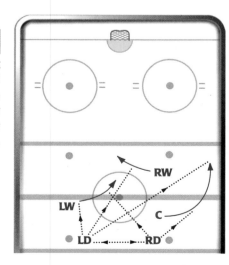

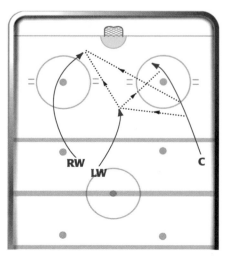

4 The Center has received the puck and carries it into the offensive zone. The RW moves wide to the left and toward the net. The LW moves to the high slot. The Center has the option of passing to either the LW or the RW. The LW, if he receives the puck, has the option of passing to either the RW or the Center.

The skating patterns of the three forwards while they are regrouping in the neutral zone.

1

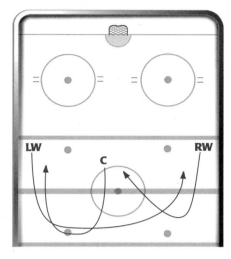

FORWARDS REGROUP (B)

The three forwards regroup in the neutral zone. This is done after the initial attempt to move into the offensive zone is stopped.

The Center has the puck and passes back to the RD. The three forwards skate their patterns.

2

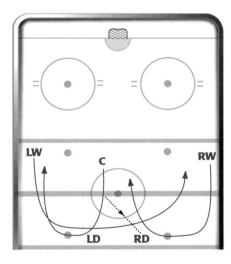

3 There are a number of possible passing plays. The RD and the LD can pass to the forwards any time during their regrouping patterns.

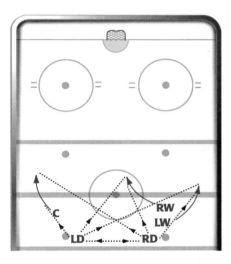

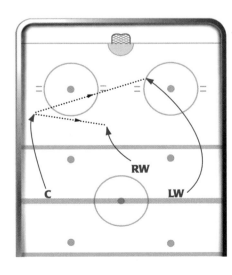

4 The Center has received the puck and carries it into the offensive zone. The LW moves along the right board deep into the zone. The RW moves up the middle toward the high slot. The Center has the option of passing to either the LW or the RW.

PLAYS

FORWARDS REGROUP (C)

The three forwards regroup in the neutral zone. This is done after the initial attempt to move into the offensive zone is stopped.

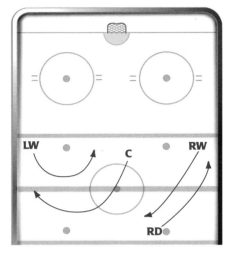

1 The skating patterns of the three forwards while they are regrouping in the neutral zone. The RD moves up into the pattern while the RW replaces the RD at his position.

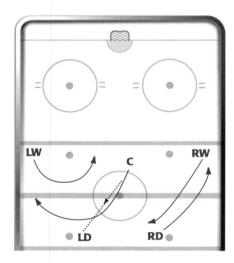

2 The Center has the puck and passes back to the LD. The forwards skate their patterns.

The LD can pass to the Center, RW, LW or RD anytime during their patterns. Also, the RW can stop and become a partner with the LD. **3**

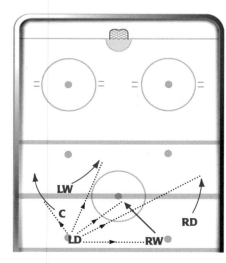

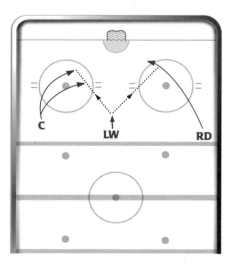

4 The LW has received the puck and carries it into the offensive zone. Both the RD and the Center stay wide and move deep into the zone. The LW has the option of passing to either the RD or the Center.

QUICK TRANSITION (A)

A defenseman gains control of the puck in the neutral zone, and the forwards quickly move to the offensive.

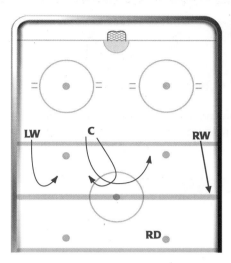

1 The first forward back to the neutral zone (RW) goes to the boards. The Center and the LW swing within their normal lanes.

2 The LD has control of the puck. He can pass to any of the forwards to start the transition.

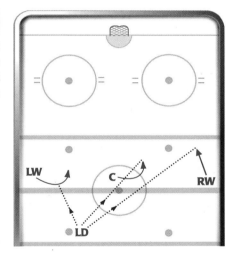

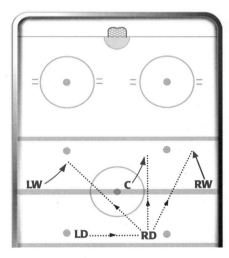

3 The LD passes to the RD, who can pass to any of the forwards to start the transition.

The transition attempts to trap the opposition's forwards (X3, X4 and X5) and to create a 3-on-2 attack.

4

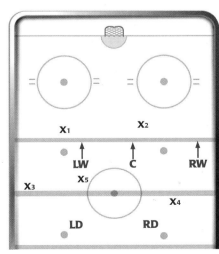

PLAYS

QUICK TRANSITION (B)

A defenseman gains control of the puck in the neutral zone, and the forwards quickly move to the offensive.

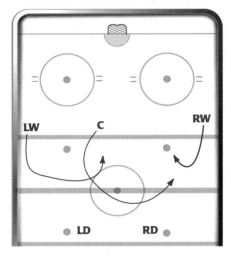

1 The first two forwards back to the neutral zone (LW and C) swing through the middle. The third forward (RW) turns and moves quickly to the blue line.

2 The LD has control of the puck. He can pass to any of the forwards to start the transition.

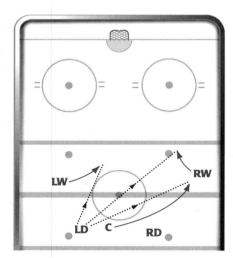

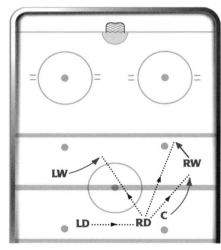

3 The LD passes to the RD, who can pass to any of the forwards to start the transition.

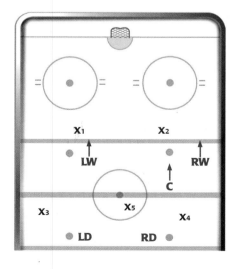

4 The transition attempts to trap the opposition's forwards (X3, X4 and X5) and to create a 3-on-2 attack.

QUICK TRANSITION (C)

A defenseman gains control of the puck in the neutral zone, and the forwards quickly move to the offensive.

1 The Center goes directly to the boards at the red line. The other two forwards (LW and RW) crisscross.

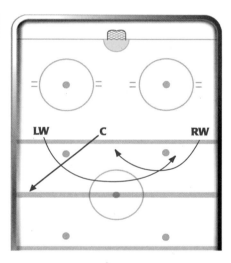

2 The LD has control of the puck. He can pass to any of the forwards to start the transition.

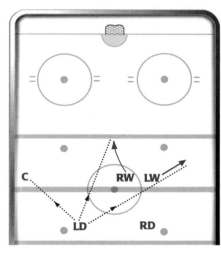

3 The LD passes to the RD, who can pass to any of the forwards to start the transition.

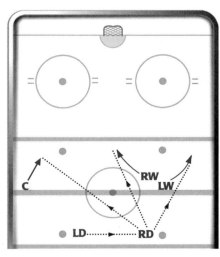

4 The transition attempts to trap the opposition's forwards (X3, X4 and X5) and to create a 3-on-2 attack.

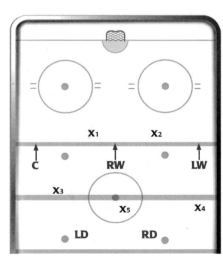

OFFENSIVE PLAY

No matter how exciting a game may be from the point of view of tactics or technique, it will not be interesting if the tactics do not result in a goal being scored.

Anatoli Tarasov
The Road to Olympus

CHAPTER SIX

OFFENSIVE ZONE PLAY

THE OBJECTIVE OF OFFENSIVE PLAY IS TO SCORE. PLAY IN THE OFFENSIVE ZONE PITS the active attackers against the reactive defense. Disciplined, systematic defenders attempt to throw up a wall around the goal, and the high-flying, creative offensive players try to break through weak spots in the fortifications. Play in the offensive zone is all about flexibility and inventiveness and creating the conditions for effective improvisation.

"Scoring in hockey demands technique plus....A game that ends 0:0 will not, I believe, be very interesting to watch. No matter how exciting a game may be from the point of view of tactics or technique, it will not be interesting if the tactics do not result in a goal being scored," wrote Anatoli Tarasov in *The Road to Olympus*.

It may seem like an obvious warning, but it is a good point nonetheless; it is possible to overplan a game of hockey, and coaches need to remember that no technique ensures a goal every time the team skates down the ice. Good offensive zone preparation is about unleashing your attackers on the opponents' goal in a way that maximizes the chances of seizing opportunities.

Offensive systems provide general guidelines to assist the team in its tactical preparation. After that, the players must be given the freedom to create and innovate.

After the rush (the initial attack), offensive zone systems allow the team to maintain or regain control of the puck and to continue the attack on the goal. Only a low percentage of goals are scored on the rush. More goals are scored after sustained pressure in the opponents' end.

Technical skills—skating, passing, stickhandling and shooting—are important on offense. Drills should be designed to incorporate the development of technical skills into the plan of attack, and drills should simulate game conditions to familiarize the players with the potential situations and the resulting opportunities.

Good offense requires a hungry, sharp-witted, tireless, clever approach to the game.

Positional Play

KEY POINTS

The Positional Play system is conservative. Its principles are basic to all offensive play. It teaches the forwards to go to the net, to attack the net. One forward is always thinking defensively, and the attack is always a controlled one because one forward has that defensive responsibility. All systems utilize the basic plays described here at various times. In this system, the wings are responsible for their respective sides and rarely cross the ice to the other side. The Center is responsible for the middle and can move to either side. This is a good system for young teams and for those with limited skating ability. Again, all teams make use of Positional Play at times, regardless of their system.

1. Positional Play is a conservative system of offense. The objectives are basic, which makes it easy to teach.

2. It stresses that one forward always be in the slot, which places him in a position to backcheck.

3. Two forwards attack the net.

4. The roles of the defensemen are conservative, but they do have the freedom to move into the high slot.

5. This system is effective when the play enters the offensive zone.

146

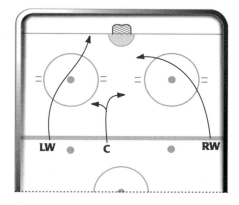

1 The two wings stay on the boards and break for the net. The Center stays in the slot.

One wing (LW) and the Center break for the net. The second wing (RW) moves to the slot. **2**

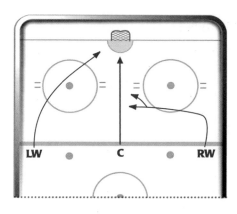

One wing (LW) goes deep in the zone toward the net. Either the second wing (RW) or the Center, usually the one who enters the zone last, stays in the slot, and the other can go deep or to the net. **3**

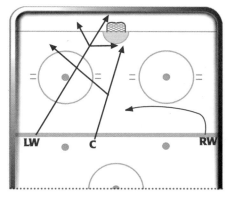

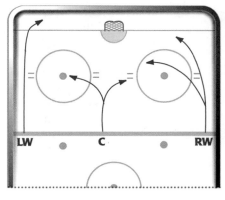

4 One wing (LW) stays along the boards and goes deep. Either the second wing (RW) or the Center, usually the one who enters the zone last, stays in the slot, and the other can go deep or to the net.

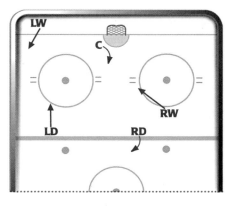

5 The defensemen are normally conservative and stay on the blue line. They are allowed to move to the high slot when the opportunity arises. When one defenseman (LD) moves in, the second defenseman (RD) moves back a few feet to cover.

DRILLS

To teach this system, specific steps should be taken to familiarize the players with the different situations. It is important that the players know their own and each other's roles. This system depends on the forward with the defensive responsibility. Offensive play must be practiced against opposition some of the time.

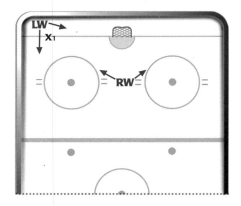

1 Many of the situations that arise during a game call for interactions between two players. Have two forwards practice working together at the different situations. For example, one wing (LW) is deep in the corner with the puck, and the second wing (RW) is in the slot. The two players work the puck toward the net. The opposition can be added, making it a 2-on-1 or 2-on-2 drill.

The different situations involving the three **2** forwards should be practiced. For example, the LW has the puck and carries it deep into the zone. The Center goes for the far post, and the RW stays in the slot. The opposition can be added, making it a 3-on-1, 3-on-2 or 3-on-3 drill.

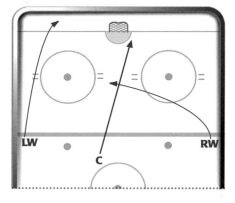

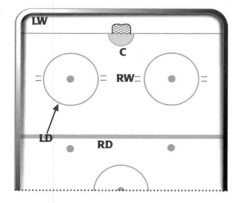

3 The above step with the addition of the defense-men increases the number of offensive situations and therefore the number of possible plays. For example, the LD can move to the top of the circle for a shot on the net. The opposition can be added to create different drills or scrimmage play.

4A

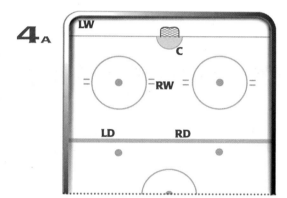

Set up the players in different situations. **4**B

By starting the play from different areas, the unit learns to interact as the position of the puck changes. If the puck is placed to the right of the goal, the Center would move to the puck and the two wings would have some choice of what to do.

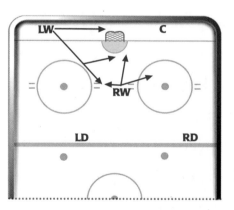

Triangular Offense

KEY POINTS

The Triangular Offense system is one that concentrates on maintaining possession of the puck. The much-used term "cycling" refers to this offense. The forwards' alignment is always some type of triangular formation, although the shape of the triangle may change. The objective is to create a 3-on-2 or, even better, a 2-on-1 situation. The triangles are employed to draw the defensemen away from the net into areas where they can be attacked by two forwards. When a defenseman moves to these areas, for instance, behind the net, along the boards near the top of the circle or in the high slot, the offensive forwards gain easier access to the net. Puck control is essential for this system, but a danger is concentrating on maintaining control of the puck and forgetting to go to the net. All teams can use this system, especially those with big forwards who have good puck-handling skills.

1. The Triangular Offense should be used when the offensive team has control of the puck and wants to maintain it.

2. The three forwards work in a triangular formation. Their movement is a result of their maneuverability relative to each other, not the movement of the puck. The movement of the puck is a result of the forwards' shifting positions.

3. The objective is to have three forwards isolate on two opposing players. The purpose is to get one forward free to make a play on the net.

4. The roles of the defensemen are conservative, but they do have the freedom to move into the high slot.

5. Puck control and passing are essential.

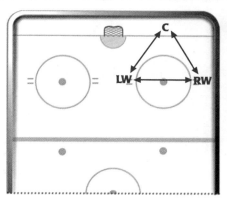

1A This formation has one forward (C) deep along the boards, a second forward (RW) along the boards and the third forward (LW) in the slot

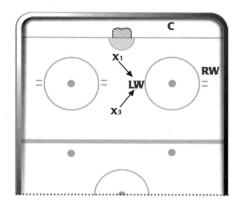

1B The position of the LW makes it difficult for the defenseman (X1) to cover him. The LW must be covered by the player responsible for the point or the player responsible for the slot. If X1 moves out, the net area is open; if X3 moves in, the point is open.

The move-ment and **1C** passwork of the triangle can put the RW in a position to go to the net or to have an open shot.

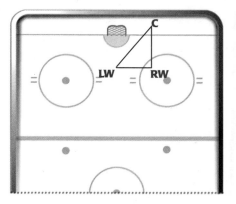

The **1D** defensemen normally are con-servative and stay on the blue line. They are allowed to move to the slot when the oppor-tunity arises. When one defenseman (RD) moves in, the second defense-man (LD) moves back a few feet to cover.

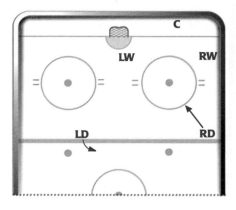

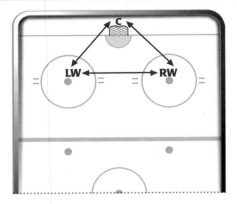

2A This formation has one forward (C) behind the net and the other two forwards (LW and RW) wide in the face-off circles.

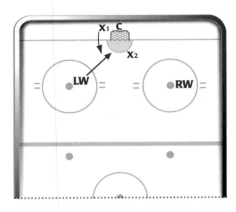

2B The defensive unit has to decide whether to pressure the Center or cover the wings. If one defenseman (X1) pressures the Center, an avenue may open for one wing to go to the net.

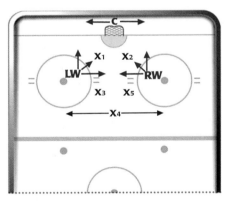

2C If the defensive unit forms a box and attempts to keep the offense to the outside, the three forwards must move short distances in an attempt to make the box move and break down. The triangle is designed to attack any breakdown.

This **3**A formation has two forwards (LW and C) behind the goal line and the third forward (RW) in the slot.

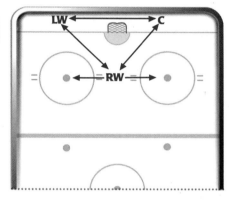

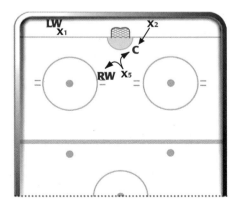

3B The two deep players attempt, through passes, to draw the defensemen away from the net. This will force a forward (X5) to cover the net area.

3C This formation forces the opposition to play many situations man-to-man. If the offensive players are able to win a 1-on-1 situation, they will have a man who is open and moves to the net. In this example, the Center has beaten X2, creating a 2-on-1 situation, with X5 forced to cover both the RW and the Center.

DRILLS

To teach this system, specific steps should be taken to familiarize the players with the different situations. This system is dependent on coordinated movement and passwork. Offensive play must be practiced against opposition some of the time.

1 The triangles should be set up. The role for each player should be explained. The players need to know their basic movement patterns and how to move and maintain the triangle.

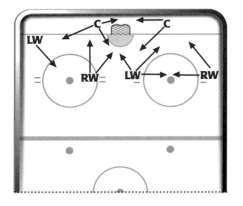

2 The triangular movement should be practiced first without pucks. This can be done either with the three forwards or the five-man offensive unit. This teaches the players to move as a reaction to the movement of the others and not as a reaction to the puck. This will be a new idea for many players.

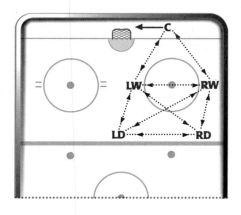

3 Introduce the pucks and practice the triangular movements. This can be done with the three forwards or the five-man offensive unit. Quick passes and short movements are essential. Passing to an open area with a player moving toward it needs to be perfected.

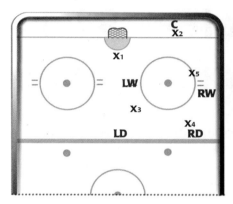

4 Introduce the opposition: first the two defensemen, then one forward followed by the two others. The different drills, such as 3-on-2 and 3-on-3, as well as scrimmage practice are covered by this step.

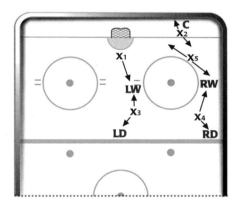

5 Review what the opposition may do to defend against the triangles. It is important for the offensive unit to know where the defensive breakdowns can occur. With this knowledge, the offensive unit will be better prepared to attack. For example, the defensive team players will attempt to restrict the triangle's movement by bringing their wings deeper into the zone. The proper adjustment by the offensive unit is to reestablish the triangle deeper in the zone.

Overload the Slot

KEY POINTS

The Overload the Slot system of offensive zone play is basic and simple. When the initial rush is unsuccessful and the follow-up attack does not result in a play on the net, the puck is moved to the points. The defensemen's jobs are to shoot the puck and to put it on the net. The forwards' jobs are to go to the net and get in position for tip-ins, deflections and rebounds. One of the objectives is for the forwards to outman the opposing defensemen in front of the net. This is a good system for teams with big forwards. Any forward with the instinct to go to the net will thrive. Courage is an important quality for the forwards to possess. This system, because much of it takes place in front of the net, is a physical one.

1. The Overload the Slot system is easy to teach, with objectives that are simple and direct.

2. Pressure is applied to the slot area with two, sometimes three, forwards playing in the slot.

3. The forwards, when in possession of the puck, control it deep. If their attempts to go to the net fail, they will move the puck to the defensemen.

4. The role for the defensemen is simple: Shoot the puck. The forwards move to the slot and net area for tip-ins, deflections and rebounds.

One forward (RW) is in the slot, and a second forward (LW) is deep along the boards. The third forward (C) plays so that he can move to the slot or deep in the zone.

1 A

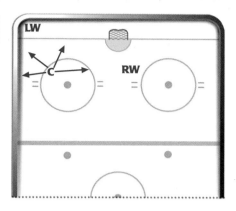

The initial attempt to make the play on the net may have the Center go to the net. This will force a defenseman (X2) to cover both the Center and the RW if the other defenseman (X1) is on the puck in the corner and if the forward (X5) does not cover the net.

1 B

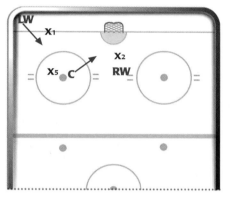

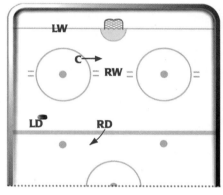

1 C If the LW makes the initial pass to the Center, he may head directly to the net. This will crowd the slot area with two offensive and two defensive players.

When the puck is moved to the defensemen, they shoot it. The forwards position themselves for tip-ins, deflections and rebounds (Diagrams 2a and 2b).

2 A

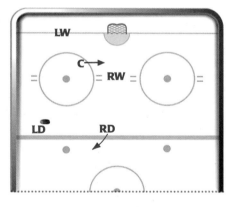

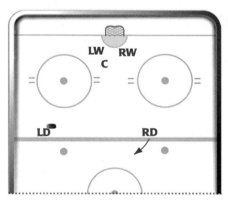

2 B

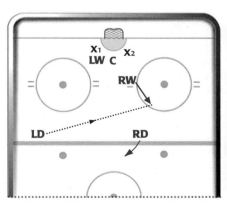

2 C An area that is often open when this system is employed is the top of the far face-off circle. The RW moves to the top of the circle while the other two forwards crowd the slot. In this case, the LD passes, rather than shoots, the puck to the RW.

DRILLS

To teach this system, specific steps should be taken to familiarize the players with the different situations. This system is dependent on the defensemen completing their roles. All offensive play must be practiced against opposition some of the time.

The role of each player **1** should be explained. The players need to know the basic movement patterns and each player's role and understand the particular importance of moving the puck to the points.

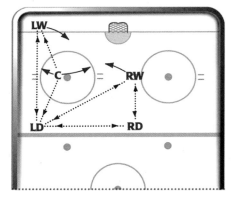

The three forwards work on **2** their basic movement patterns without pucks. The five-man unit works on the basic movement patterns as well. Among other things, this teaches the players to go to the net.

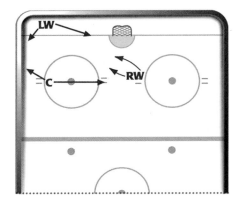

3 Introduce the puck first with the entire five-man unit.

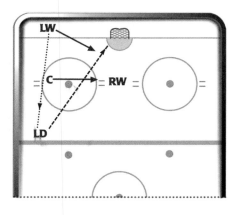

4 A shooting drill with the forwards moving into the slot area for tip-ins, deflections and rebounds teaches the unit quick execution. Stationary objects, such as chairs or traffic cones, can be used to simulate the opposition's defensemen.

The opposition is inserted. The two **5** defensemen are first, then one forward followed by the other two. The different drills, such as 3-on-2 and 3-on-3, as well as scrimmage practice are covered by this step.

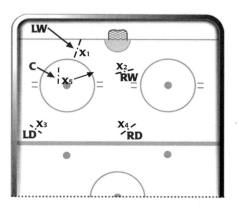

6 Review what the opposition may do to defend against this system. It is important that the offensive unit recognizes the defensive setup in order to prevent the system's major risk—the three forwards being trapped—from happening. Wings will check defensemen closer. All three forwards go to the net.

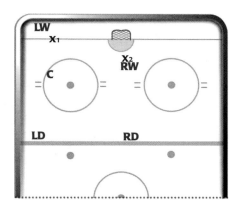

SECTION THREE

SPECIAL TEAM PLAY

THE RULES OF THE GAME MAKE "SPECIAL SITUATIONS" A CRUCIAL PART OF hockey. Play moves quickly, penalties are assessed regularly, and they often play an important part in determining the winners and losers. When one team has a player advantage, the other has a player disadvantage. Every power play must be met with penalty killing, and a team that can dominate in these special circumstances usually has a good chance of winning.

The same applies to face-offs. Every time the play stops, there is an opportunity to grab the tempo away from the opposition and to move onto the offensive.

No coach can afford to ignore these situations. Practices must include enough time to cover them, because when you count up the number of times they occur during a game, the importance of preparing for face-offs and penalties becomes obvious.

The game of hockey has room for specialists. Every team can use a centerman with enough quickness and hand-eye coordination to win a high percentage of his draws. A player with limited offensive skills, but with a sound understanding of the game can become an excellent penalty killer. A player with quick hands but little aptitude for physical play can become a goal scorer in those open-ice power play situations.

Not only are coaches wise to emphasize player specialization, but doing so is a gratifying part of the job. All players want to contribute to their team's success, and having a special skill recognized and put to use makes any player happy.

SPECIAL TEAM PLAY

It is the sum total of the entire unit that counts, not the total of any one part. I must be patient first in my evaluation and then in my selection.

John Wooden
They Call Me Coach

CHAPTER SEVEN

POWER PLAYS

THE IMPORTANCE OF THE POWER PLAY HAS GROWN IN RECENT YEARS, AND successful teams are usually ranked among the clubs with the best man-advantage records. Power play opportunities cannot be consistently squandered if a team is to succeed.

Proper coaching is critical for the power play. Sure, it helps to have skilled players, but it still comes down to teamwork and execution. Enough practice time is needed to perfect the power play; all teams should work on the power play at most practices. This usually takes place with one coach and a few players. The other players are working on something else with the other coaches in the other zones.

Power plays are not complicated or complex; in fact, the opposite is true. They are simple, designed to concentrate on two or three areas. Only a few options exist for any power play, and it is the execution that is vital. Power plays start with a 5-on-4 situation. The objective is to eliminate the penalty killers; in essence, to go from a 5-on-4 to a 3-on-2 to a 2-on-1 to a 1-on-0.

Power play personnel are a key to success. There must be a comfortable fit between the personnel and the type of power play used, and it is important for the coach to know his players and their abilities when selecting a power play. Usually, the players with the better skills are on the power play; however, there are enough different power plays to accommodate different styles of players or combinations of the different styles.

Nine power plays are presented here. The first three, the Funnel, the 2-1-2 and the Defensemen Slide, include a suggested step-by-step teaching approach. The coach needs to understand the options for each power play to be able to decide if he has the right players to do the job.

The Funnel

KEY POINTS

The Funnel power play is a conservative one with limited options. The primary play is to have the defensemen shoot the puck and have the forwards in position for tip-ins, deflections and rebounds. A second option has a forward move away from the net into a face-off circle for a pass. This power play favors big players with the knack for scoring from close range. The forwards must have the courage to play in front of the net and take a pounding.

1. The Funnel is a simple power play with limited options available.

2. The objective is to have the defensemen shoot and the three forwards outman the opposition's defensemen for position in front of the net.

3. When entering the offensive zone, the power play should be set up deep in the zone. The initial passes are made to open the points prior to moving the puck to the defensemen.

The power play takes **1** place in a funnel-shaped area. It goes from the points at the boards to the goal posts.

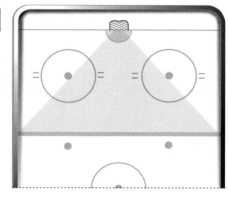

2 Proper Alignment. The three forwards are in the slot, and the defensemen play normal positions on the blue line.

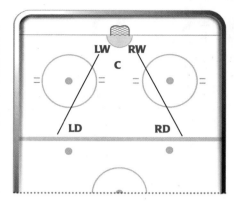

Basic Alignment. 3 When the puck is on the boards, the LD has the puck and the RW moves out away from the net.

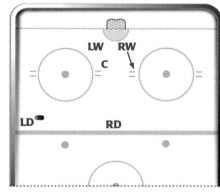

4 This power play works because the defensemen are usually open at the point to initiate a new move or shot to the net. For example, if one forward (LW) has the puck and he cannot get it to the other two forwards (C and RW), he can look to the defensemen.

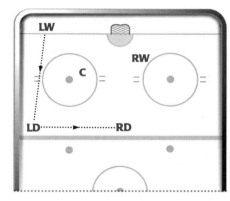

When the puck **5** moves to the defensemen, the three forwards move to the front of the net. The opposition's defensemen will then be outmanned 3-on-2. The forwards must be in position for tip-ins, deflections and rebounds.

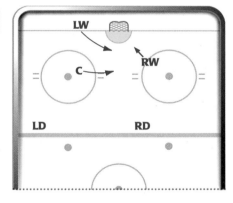

6 A second play has the LD with the puck along the boards. The off-wing (RW) moves away from the net area into the face-off circle, which creates a passing option.

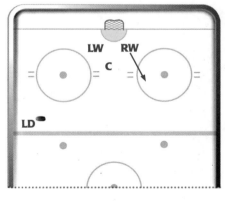

This power play normally **7** emphasizes direct shots on the net, but the RW, by moving away from the net and the penalty killers, becomes open. The LD passes to the RW in the opposite face-off circle.

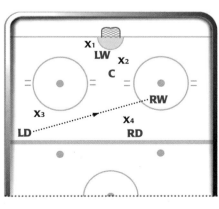

8 The RW can shoot, which is the high-percentage play, or he can pass to the LW or Center, who may be open as a result of the opposition's reaction to the LD's pass.

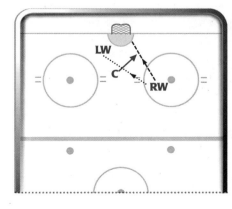

165

DRILLS

Coaches teaching the Funnel should emphasize the rough-and-tumble nature of this system and the importance of getting in position for tip-ins and rebounds.

1 A complete explanation of the power play, its formation, movement patterns and options, is the initial step. Each player must know his role, the roles of the others and how the roles are related.

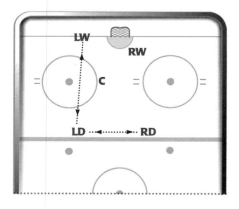

2 The power play formation should be set up. The passwork should be quick and crisp. Isolate on different pass routes; for instance, the LW to the LD, and the LD to the RD. Passwork must be perfected. This step should include player movement as well.

3 The defensemen have to develop hard and accurate shots. Drills that emphasize receiving a pass and shooting quickly are important. For example, have one forward (LW) pass the puck to the LD, who either shoots or passes to the RD, who then shoots.

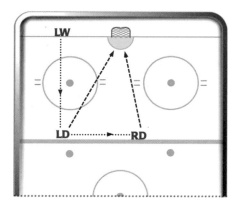

The three forwards move **4** into position after the defenseman (LD) receives a pass. This drill is tough on goalies, and the participation of a goalie is optional.

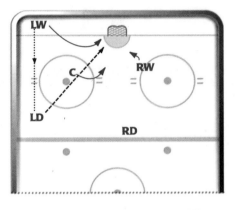

Place stationary **5** objects at strategic defensive locations. This makes optimal use of the limited time available to practice the execution of the power play.

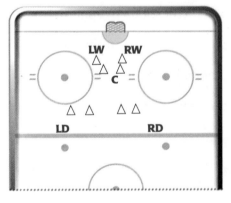

6 Introduce the penalty-killing unit. Be sure to use both a tight and a wide box. This teaches the power play unit to react to the different defenses. This step should be done with quickness and tempo.

2 - 1 - 2

KEY POINTS

The 2-1-2 power play has great flexibility. The options can emphasize the forwards or the defensemen or both. It can set up deep in the zone, along the blue line or from the boards. The ultimate option is to get the puck to the man in the slot, the "1" man in the 2-1-2 alignment. Another option has the forwards concentrate on the two defensemen. Another is to have the defensemen shoot the puck (similar to the funnel). Passwork is the important skill for this power play. A team needs to have players with effective passing and stickhandling skills to use this power play.

1. The 2-1-2 is a balanced power play that works from either the front "2" (forwards) or the back "2" (defensemen).

2. The objective is to get the puck to the man in the slot, who can make a play on the net.

3. There are numerous options available in this power play.

4. When entering the offensive zone, the power play should be set up deep in the zone.

Proper Alignment. **1** Two forwards (LW and RW) are deep in the zone, and one forward (C) is in the slot. The defensemen play normal positions on the blue line.

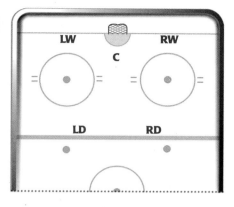

If the play shifts to the **2** boards, a similar alignment is used. The 2-1-2 formation remains constant.

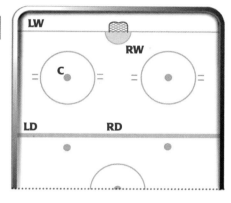

3 The three forwards have room to move without altering the basic alignment. The deep forwards have more freedom to move and redirect the power play than does the forward in the slot.

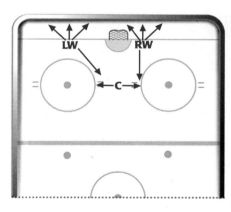

4 The defensemen (LD and RD) can move along the blue line, and the forwards must adjust.

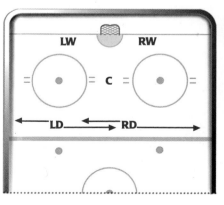

The LD and the RD can **5** pass between each other. The two deep forwards (LW and RW) can move about to create openings.

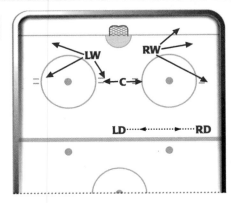

6 The primary objective of this power play is to get the puck to the man in the slot. The basic passing patterns involve one defenseman (LD), one deep forward (LW) and the forward in the slot (C).

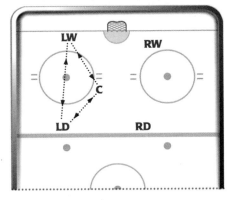

7 The same play can be executed from the other side when the puck is passed to the RD. The Center just has to move a couple of strides across the slot.

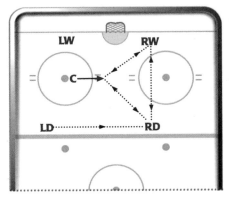

The RW is in **8** a position that allows the LD to pass directly to him if the penalty-killing unit plays too loose. If this is done, it creates a 3-on-2 situation. The three forwards can then attack the net.

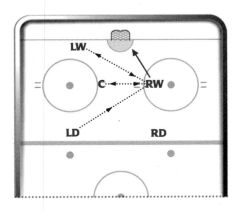

9 The defensemen have the option of shooting the puck. The three forwards are in positions that allow them to quickly converge on the net for tip-ins, deflections and rebounds.

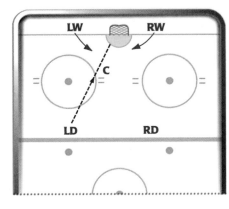

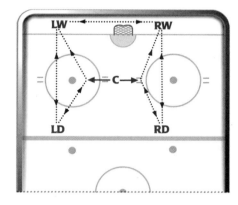

10 The two deep forwards (LW and RW) can move deep behind the goal line. This enables the offensive unit to stretch its passing patterns over more of the offensive zone.

Moving the deep **11** forwards to behind the goal line forces the defensive unit to spread out. The play is then to get the puck to the Center in the slot.

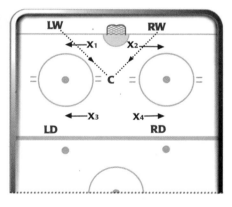

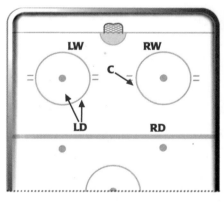

12 Another play has a defenseman (LD) move in to the top of the face-off circle. The Center can stay in the slot or move to the other face-off circle.

When the **13** LD moves into the face-off circle, he becomes a prime offensive player. He may be open for passes from the other players. He can shoot or pass to one of the forwards if one is open.

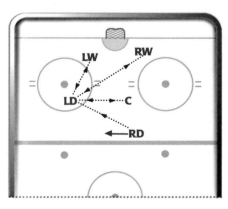

DRILLS

Coaches should emphasize that the 2-1-2 is about passing and getting the puck to the "1" man in front of the net.

1 Begin with a complete explanation of the power play, its formation, movement patterns and options. Each player must know his role, the roles of the others and how the roles are related.

Set up the power play formation. The passwork should be quick and crisp. Isolate on different pass routes; for instance, the Center to the LW, the LW to the LD, and the LD to the RD. The passwork must be perfected. This step should include movement as well. **2**

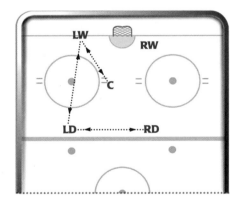

3 The forward in the slot (C) is the main scoring threat. To teach him the proper position from which to shoot quickly, have him receive passes from the LD and the LW and then shoot without delay. The drill should have the LD and the LW alternate passes.

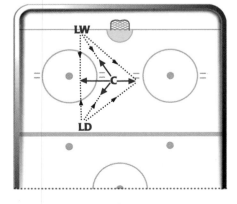

4 Practice the specific plays. The drills need to result in a play on the net. Emphasize the need to do it at top speed: pass, pass, shot.

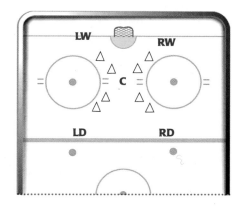

5 Place stationary objects at strategic defensive locations. This optimizes the limited time available to practice the execution of the power play.

6 Introduce the penalty-killing unit. Be sure to use both a tight and a wide box. This teaches the power play unit to react to the different defenses. This step should be done with quickness and tempo.

Defensemen Slide

KEY POINTS

The Defensemen Slide power play emphasizes the points. The options are derived from the defensemen moving across (sliding) the blue line. It helps to have the defensemen play their off-sides to enhance their passing angles. Several options become available. One is to draw the penalty killer across as the defensemen slide, then pass back across to a forward. He, in turn, with a second forward, attacks the defenseman 2-on-1. A second option has the defensemen pass to the off-side wing, who becomes a "shooter." A team needs to have talented defensemen who can move laterally quickly and are adept at handling the puck. The defensemen must "see the ice" as well. This power play is dependent on passwork and player movement.

1. The Defensemen Slide power play focuses on the defensemen, who normally slide across the blue line.

2. The objective is to trick the penalty killers covering the points into moving out of position and thus creating a 3-on-2 situation.

3. The forwards, with proper movement, try to reduce the 3-on-2 to a 2-on-1 to an open man on the net.

4. There are numerous options available within this system.

5. When entering the offensive zone, the power play should be set up either deep in the zone or midway along the boards.

Proper Alignment. One forward (LW) is deep in the zone, a second forward (C) is on the boards, and the third forward (RW) is wide in the area of the face-off circle. The defensemen play normal positions on the blue line.

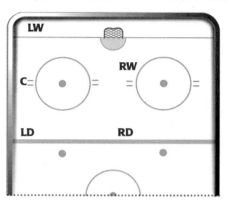

The three forwards have room to move without altering the basic alignment. The RW, in particular, has the most freedom to move and redirect the power play. The LW and the Center normally move in tandem, reacting to each other.

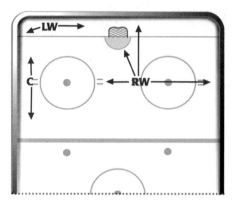

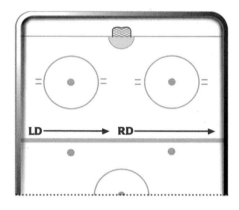

The defensemen (LD and RD) have freedom to move along the blue line.

The primary play in this power play has the two defensemen slide across the blue line. This is done to draw the penalty killers across as well. The Center moves back toward the blue line and is in a position to take a pass from the LD.

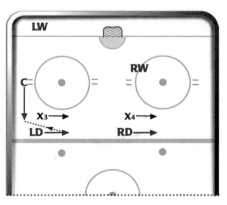

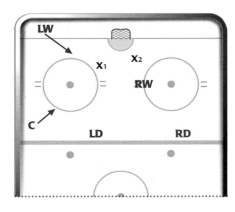

5 When the Center receives the puck, he moves quickly toward the net to create a 3-on-2 situation. This forces the opposition's puck-side defenseman (X1) to cover both the Center and the LW.

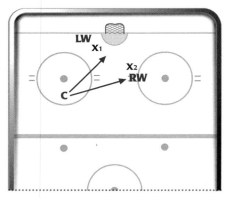

6 If X1 covers the LW, the Center has the option of going directly to the net or making a play with the RW. The RW can also screen out X2, giving the Center open access to the net.

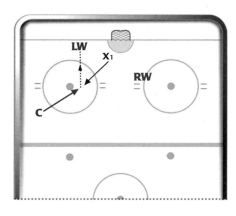

7 If X1 covers the Center, the Center passes to the LW, who goes to the net.

If X2 moves to cover the **8** LW, the RW becomes the open man in front of the net .

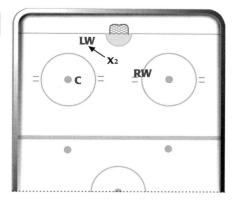

The RW is in a position **9** that allows the LD and the Center to pass to him. This is important if the penalty killers play in a wide formation. If such a pass is successful, it opens up a direct play on the net. This is an example of the options available in addition to the play from the points.

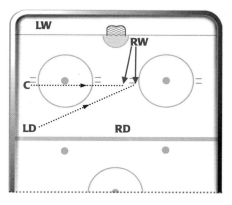

Alternatively, **10** the Center can pass the puck back to the LD, who has moved inside X3.

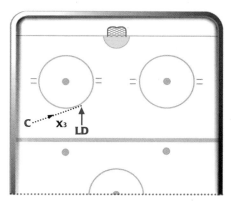

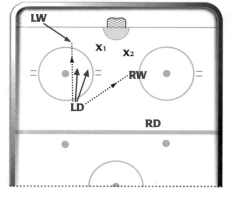

11 The LD has the option of keeping the puck or passing to the LW or the RW. This creates a 3-on-2 against X1 and X2.

DRILLS

Coaches should emphasize that the Defensemen Slide system relies on drawing opponents out of position and opening up a "shooter" to receive a pass.

1 Begin with a complete explanation of the power play, its formation, movement patterns and options. Each player must know his role, the roles of the others and how the roles are related.

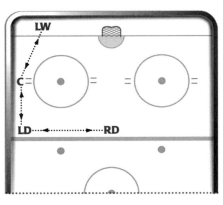

2 Set up the power play formation, then practice making the passwork quick and crisp. Isolate on different pass routes; for instance, the LW to the Center, the LD to the RD, and the LD to the Center. Include player movement as well.

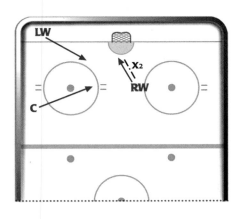

3 Teach the off-side wing (RW) the proper technique for screening. A drill that accomplishes this has the RW move in front of X2 as either the LW or the Center goes to the net. The RW must do this with a minimal amount of clutching or hooking.

The specific **4**
plays should be
practiced. The plays
should work the
puck to an open man
in front of the net.
Emphasize the need
to accomplish this at
top speed.

Place stationary **5**
objects at
strategic defensive
locations to make the
most of the available
practice time.

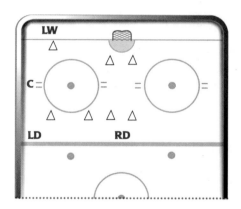

Introduce the **6**
penalty-killing
unit. Be sure to use both
a tight and a wide box
so that you teach the
power play unit to react
to different defenses.
This step should be
done with quickness
and tempo.

Wings Play the Off-Side

KEY POINTS

The Wings Play the Off-Side power play focuses on the alignment of the players. The wings play the off-side; for instance, the LW is a right shot, and the RW is a left shot. The wings see more of the ice, have better passing angles and can "one-touch" shoot the puck with this alignment. The positioning has the wings spread wide, with the Center down deep in the zone. The first option is to move the puck to the wings, who shoot. The Center's role is primarily that of a playmaker. Teams that use this power play must have forwards who can one-touch shoot the puck.

1. The wings play the off-side.

2. The primary objective of this power play is to get the wings open for a shot.

3. The Center is primarily a playmaker. He plays deep in the zone and is able to move to the net quickly.

4. The defensemen are secondary shooters.

5. When entering the offensive zone, the puck should be set up on the "strong side," that is, the side containing three offensive players.

Basic Alignment. The wings (LW and RW) are spread apart. The Center is deep in the zone, and the defensemen (RD and LD) play normal positions.

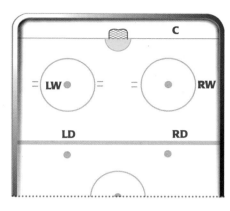

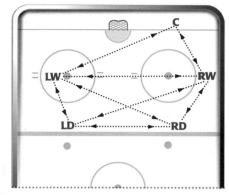

The alignment of the players permits a number of different passing avenues.

Player movement on the weak side (LW and LD), coupled with puck movement on the strong side (RW, C and RD), is the key to creating an open man for a shot.

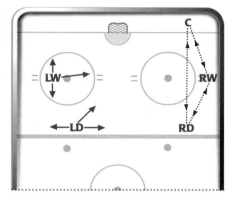

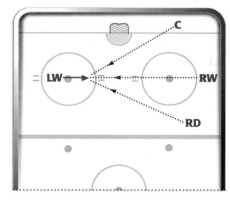

Play 1. The primary play is to get the LW open for a shot. Normally, this is done with a pass from the strong side (RW, C or RD).

In order for the LW to be open, the penalty killer (X3) has to be forced out of position.

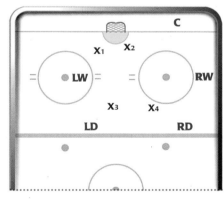

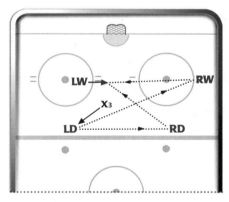

This is best done when the LD passes quickly to the RW or the RD, who, in turn, passes to the LW. The LW moves to the slot area before X3 can get back to cover.

Play 2. A second play is to have the RW shift if the penalty killer X4 is out of position. X4's bad positioning (crowding the RD too closely) allows the RW to move to the slot and receive a pass from the LD, the LW or the Center.

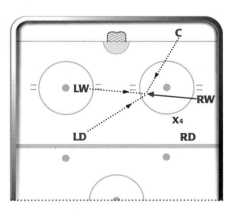

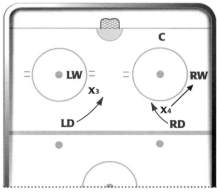

Play 3. A third possible play is to have a defenseman (LD) move into a position to shoot. Then if X3 checks the LD too closely or if X4 checks the RW too closely, the defenseman (RD) is able to move to a high-percentage shot area.

1 - 2 - 2

KEY POINTS

The 1-2-2 power play focuses on the alignment of the players. The initial alignment, with the wings wide and the Center deep, utilizes most of the offensive zone. The three forwards are spread farther apart than in the Wings Play the Off-Side power play. The purpose of this alignment is to force the defensive unit to spread out. The options are determined by the penalty-killing unit. If the penalty-killing box stays tight, the power play moves the puck around the outside for a shot. If the box spreads out, the power play will go down deep in the zone and attack the two defensemen. To make either option work, this power play must have players who can pass the puck as well as carry it while moving around small areas.

1. The 1-2-2 power play utilizes much of the offensive zone with its spread-out alignment.

2. The Center usually plays the deep position and is able to quarterback the play from there.

3. The wings play spread out.

4. The defensemen play a spread-out position.

5. The tactical approach is flexible. The power play unit reacts to the penalty killers' alignment.

6. When entering the offensive zone, the puck should be set up deep in the zone.

Proper Alignment.
The Center is deep near the net. The wings (LW and RW) are spread far apart, and the defensemen (LD and RD) play a wide position. With each play, the formation collapses toward the front of the net. If the play on the net is unsuccessful, the formation opens out again. **1**

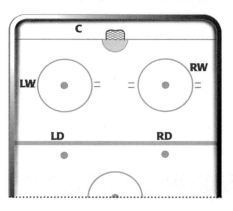

The forwards have a number of possible movements they can make without changing the basic alignment. **2**

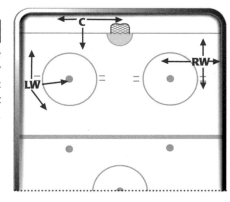

3 If penalty killers use a wide box to defend against the 1-2-2, the normal tactic will be to keep the puck deep, with the forwards (LW, C and RW) attacking X1 and X2.

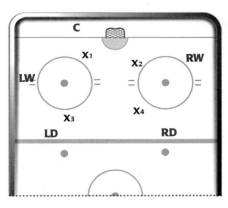

PLAYS

1-2-2

Play 1. **1**A
The Center passes to the LW and moves to the slot. The RW simultaneously moves to the net.

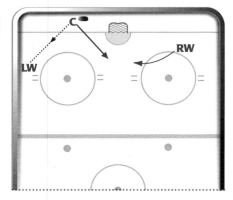

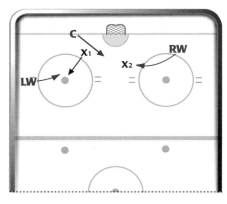

1B The LW moves toward the slot. If X1 moves to the LW, the Center and the RW have to be covered by X2. The LW can shoot or pass to the RW or the Center.

Play 2. **2**A
The Center passes to the LW, who has moved into the face-off circle. The RW simultaneously moves to the slot.

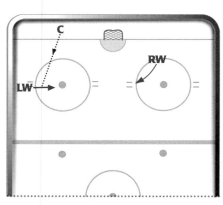

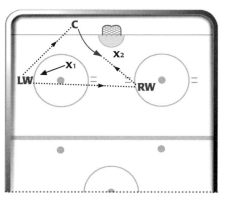

2B If X1 moves to the LW, the LW can pass directly to the Center or to the RW, who then passes to the Center.

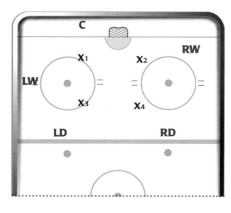

2C If the penalty killers use a tight box to defend against the 1-2-2, the normal tactic will be to use all five players and attempt to free one for a shot.

Play 3.
The Center 3A passes to the LW, who passes to the LD.

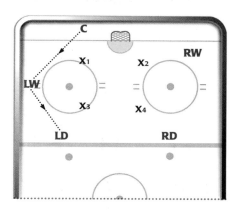

The LW moves to 3B the slot, the Center to the face-off circle and the RW to the slot.

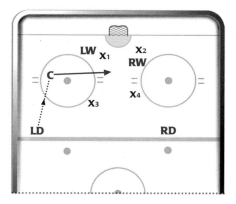

The LD passes to the Center. 3C The Center can shoot or move to the net and make a play to the RW or the LW if they are open.

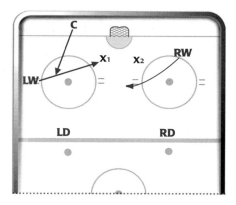

Either the RW or the LW is 3D in a position to pick off a penalty killer. For example, the LW can pick off X1 and allow the Center and the RW to attack X2 2-on-1.

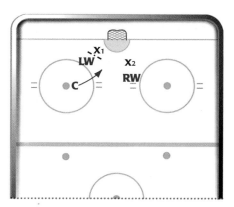

185

Man in Front of the Net

KEY POINTS

Man in Front of the Net power play may be the simplest of all. It has one forward—usually a big, tough, physical forward—constantly play in front of the net. He does this partly to harass the defensemen and goalie and partly to be in position for loose pucks, tip-ins, deflections and rebounds. The options for this one revolve around the other two forwards and the defensemen shooting the puck. The primary skill is shooting the puck. This power play is for teams with size and players who have limited skills.

1. The Man in Front of the Net power play is basic: one forward is always in front of the net.

2. With one forward in front of the net, the other two forwards are free to move about in the offensive zone.

3. The defensemen play a normal position.

4. The plays are simple. The main objective is to outplay the defensive unit in the net area.

5. When entering the offensive zone, the puck can be set up deep or at the blue line.

Proper Alignment. **1** One forward (RW) is in front of the net. The Center and the LW play deep, with freedom to move about. The defensemen (LD and RD) play normal positions.

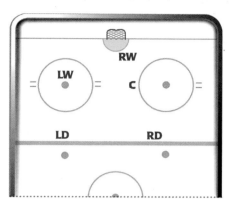

2 The objective of this power play is to outplay the opposition in the net area. The three forwards are aggressive against X1 and X2.

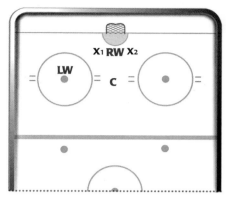

Play 1. **3A** The LW has the puck and passes to the LD. The LD can pass back to the LW or to the Center in the slot area.

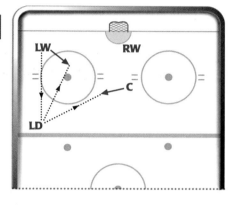

3B The LW and the Center can pass between each other or shoot. The RW is in position to screen a defender (X2) as well as for a rebound or tip-in.

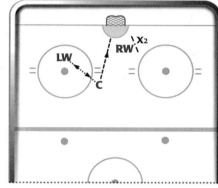

Play 2. **4A** The LW passes to the LD, who passes quickly back to the LW. The LW then passes to the RD.

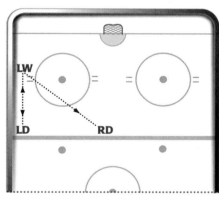

4B The RD has the option of shooting, if open, or passing to the LW or the Center.

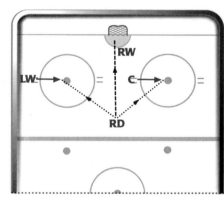

The LW, the **4C** Center and the RW attack X1 and X2 in a 3-on-2 situation.

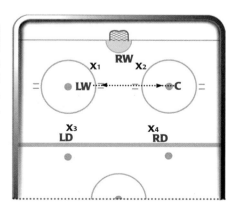

From the Corner

KEY POINTS

The From the Corner power play focuses on its place of origin, the corner. The options are directed from the corner, and the power play unit initially sets up with the puck in the corner. Whenever it needs to regain positional control, one player controls the puck in the corner. The primary option is to keep the puck deep and attack the defensemen. A second option is to get the puck to the points if one of the penalty-killing forwards moves in deep to help his defensemen. Teams that use this power play must have at least two forwards who are capable of controlling the puck deep in the corner and quarterbacking it from there.

1. The From the Corner power play originates in the corner and plays aggressively deep for the most part.

2. One forward is responsible for setting up in the corner to start the play. This is done with the belief that the opposition will not break the box to go into the corner.

3. The other forwards have freedom to move about.

4. The defensemen play normal positions, but either may move onto the offensive.

5. The primary objective is always to play 3-on-2 against the penalty-killing unit's two defensemen and, if possible, to slide a defenseman deep to create a 4-on-2 situation.

Proper Alignment. 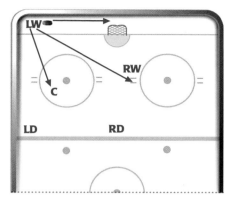 One forward (LW) sets up in the corner with the puck, and the other two forwards (RW and C) play normal positions, with freedom to move about. The defensemen (LD and RD) play normal positions. The direction of the power play is always from the corner and to the net or slot area. For the most part, the puck remains deep in the zone.

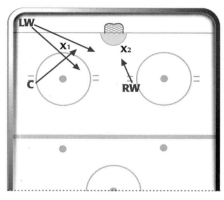 **2** This power play puts constant pressure on the opposition's defensemen (X1 and X2).

Play 1. **3** The simplest play is for the three forwards to attack X1 and X2. For example, the Center moves to the net, the RW moves across the slot, and the LW, with the puck, moves out of the corner. The Center attempts to screen X2, and the LW and the RW attack X1 (who will have moved to the front of the net) in a 2-on-1 situation. Ideally, the RW has a play on net.

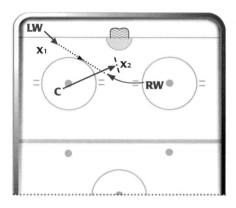

Play 2. **4A** A second play has the LW in the corner with the puck. The RW goes behind the net for a pass, and the Center moves either to the net or to the slot area. The LD slides into the area at the top of the face-off circle.

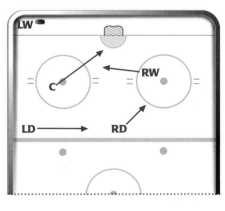

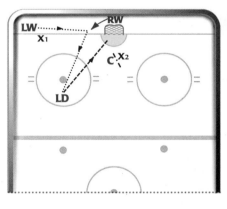 **4B** The resulting play could be a pass from the LW to the RW, who, in turn, passes to the LD, who is open for a shot.

Play 3. **5A** Another play has the Center move to the net. The RW moves into the slot, and the RD moves to the top of the face-off circle. The LD moves to the middle of the blue line to cover, and the LW has the puck in the corner.

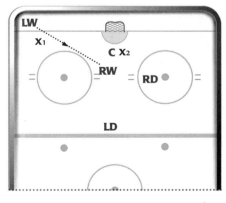

5B The initial play could be for the LW to pass to the RW in the slot. This would put three players (RW, C and RD) against X2.

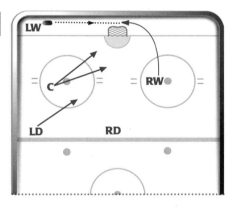

189

Czech Power Play

KEY POINTS

The Czech Power Play stresses flexibility to decide the available options. It is called this because it was used by the Czech national teams for years. The wings play the off-side; that is, the LW shoots right, and the RW shoots left. It works equally well deep in the zone or from the blue line. One option is to create a 3-on-2 situation, either with three forwards or two forwards and a defenseman, and attack the two defensemen. The second option is to have a defenseman move to the top of the circle and one-touch shoot the puck. A third option is to get the puck to the off-side wing, who one-touch shoots the puck. Teams need to have skilled players with quick reflexes who have sound puck-handling skills as well as good mobility to use this power play.

1. The Czech Power Play is flexible. It has a number of plays that can be effective with direction both from the forwards and from the defensemen.

2. At least one forward plays deep near the goal or behind the goal line. The other forwards play either in the slot area or one deep and one in the slot.

3. The defensemen play close together toward the middle of the blue line.

4. The primary objective of this power play is to work from a 5-on-4 to a 2-on-1 or, even better, a 1-on-0.

Proper Alignment. One forward, in this example the Center, is in deep near the net. The other two forwards (LW and RW) are wide in the face-off circles. The defensemen (LD and RD) are fairly close together toward the middle of the blue line.

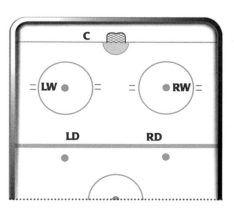

This alignment has a number of passing routes. A key avenue is between the two defensemen. They will pass the puck back and forth in an effort to get the penalty killers to maintain a wide box. This gives the forwards more room.

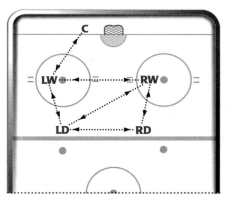

PLAYS

CZECH POWER PLAY

Play 1.
This play is a simple 3-on-2 against the defensemen (X1 and X2). For example, the LW passes to the Center and moves to the net to pick X2. The RW moves across the slot for a pass from the Center.

1 **A**

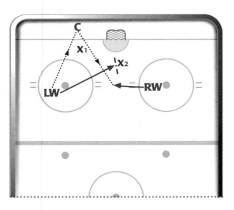

1 **B** Another option for this play is to have the LD move to the top of the face-off circle. The Center can pass to the LD, who either shoots or passes to the RW, who has held his position. This play often originates at the blue line, with the LD passing to the LW.

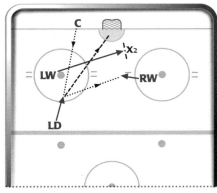

Play 2.
A second play is the cross-ice pass to the off-wing. The RD and LD have passed the puck back and forth. The penalty killers X3 and X4 have moved out to the blue line. The RW moves back to the top of the face-off circle. The LD passes to the RW.

2 **A**

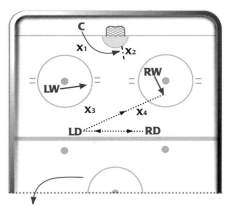

2 **B** The RW can shoot, move to the slot or play a 3-on-2 with the Center and the LW against X1 and X2.

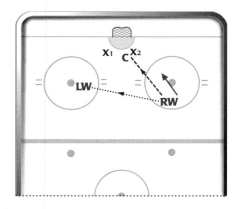

Play 3. A third play is a screen. The Center moves inside X1 and screens him out. This allows the LW and the RW to attack X2 in a 2-on-1 situation.

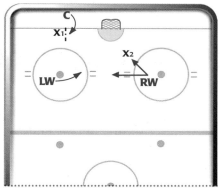

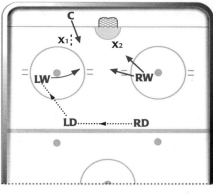

For example, the puck is at the blue line. The LD passes to the LW. The Center has moved inside of X1 and blocked his path to the front of the net. The LW and the RW move to the net against X2.

Play 4. This play has one forward use the net as a screen. The puck is on the left side. The RW skates behind the net, and the Center moves to the slot. The RD moves to the top of the face-off circle. The play depends on the opposition's defensemen (X1 and X2) ignoring the RW.

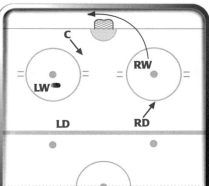

The LW, the LD and the RD pass the puck between themselves. The Center has moved to the slot/net area. The RW moves (literally sneaks) in behind the Center and takes a pass from the LW. The RW shoots on the net. The pass to the RW may come from the RD if the alignment permits it.

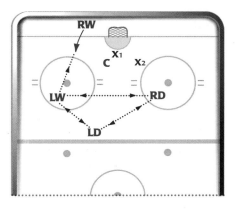

Diamond Formation

KEY POINTS

The Diamond Formation power play has a 2-2-1 alignment, with a defenseman as the "1." The primary option is to have the "1" shoot the puck and the deeper twosome go to the net. Passing is the critical skill for this power play. The players, once in this alignment, have limited room to move around. It is the passwork that forces the penalty-killing unit to get out of position and free up the "1" for the shot. This power play is a good option to work within many of the other power plays. Teams must have players who can pass the puck for this power play.

1. The 2-2-1 formation comprises two sets of forwards and one defenseman.

2. Passwork is important for the success of this power play.

3. The four forwards are all primary shooters when they become open.

4. The defenseman can be a shooter but is more often a playmaker.

5. This power play is balanced. It can work from either the right or the left side.

Proper Alignment. **1**
Two forwards (LW and C) are deep. The third forward (RW) and a defenseman (LD) are the second pair and are near or in the face-off circles. The RD is the only defenseman on the blue line.

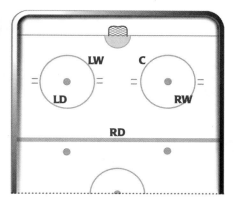

2 The opposition usually counters with a wide box that plays the four players in the zone man-to-man. The RD is therefore often left alone in the middle of the blue line. There are a number of passing avenues.

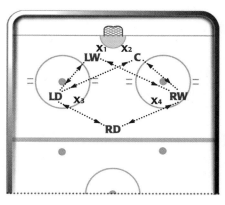

Play 1. **3A**
The RD has the puck. He may shoot, though it is a low-percentage shot. If a penalty killer (X4) moves to him, he passes to the RW.

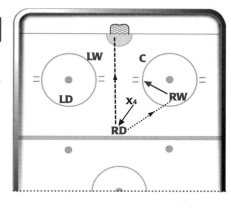

3B The RW moves to the net in a 3-on-2 situation with the LW and Center.

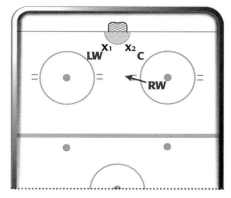

Play 2. **4A**
A second play has the RD, the LD and the LW passing on one side. If neither the LW nor the LD is able to get to the net, the RW can move to the slot for a pass from the LW.

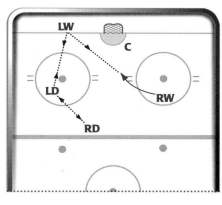

4B Another option has the LD moving back toward the board, drawing X3 with him. This permits the RD to move into the high slot for a pass from the LD. The RD now has a high-percentage shot if he chooses to shoot.

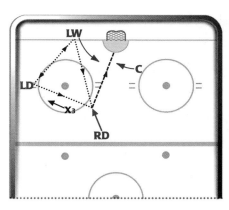

Play 3. **5A**
A third play has the two deep forwards (LW and C) move behind the goal line. This usually forces the penalty killers' box to move in farther. The RD can move in off the blue line for a pass from either the LD or the RW.

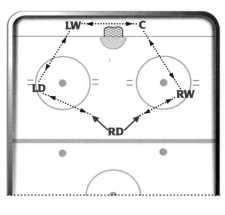

5B Often a penalty killer (X4) moves to the RD. The RW becomes open and can move into the slot. The RW can take a pass from the RD, the LD or the LW.

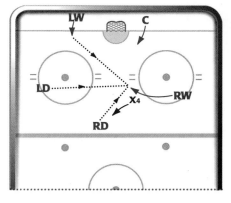

SPECIAL TEAM PLAY

All players want to contribute to their team's success, and having a special skill recognized and put to use makes any player happy.

Michael A. Smith

CHAPTER EIGHT

PENALTY KILLING

A TEAM'S ABILITY TO KILL OFF PENALTIES IS EVERY BIT AS IMPORTANT AS ITS ABILITY to score when it is on the power play. Yet when special situations are considered, coaches too often place all the emphasis on power play skills. Effective penalty killing negates the opposition's best scoring opportunities and enables your team to return to even strength full of confidence. The ideal is to have good power play skills *and* sound penalty killing; teams with both will usually be successful.

Penalty killing is an extension of a team's defensive play. Whether aggressive, conservative or a combination of both, a team's defensive style should be reflected in its penalty-killing tactics. A team with good speed can attack the puck in the offensive zone, while a team that has size is more likely to stress disciplined play in its own end. As in all other systems, the abilities of team personnel decide how the coach should proceed.

Penalty killing, even more than normal defense, is a matter of reacting to the puck and the offensive team's alignment. Yes, the defensive strategy is important, and teams must have penalty-killing plans, but more than anything else, capable penalty killing requires quick, intelligent reaction.

In the offensive zone, the penalty-killing units have some room for creativity and aggressive pursuit, but as the play moves into the neutral zone, the checking becomes closer and more methodical. With fewer defenders available, it becomes all the more crucial that the offense not be given opportunities to capitalize on a defender's mistake. In the defensive zone, the focus is on disciplined play intended either to gain possession of the puck or simply to clear the zone. A coach must constantly remind penalty killers that possession does not need to result in an effective breakout. Players must never hesitate to ice the puck.

It is difficult to practice killing penalties. Certainly, one way to do so is in a scrimmage situation against the power play unit. In general, however, this is an area that relies on the coach's ability to communicate ideas.

0 - 4

KEY POINTS

The 0-4 is a conservative system. It does not forecheck or pressure the puck in the offensive zone. It permits the power play to clear its zone with little resistance. The resistance, if any, comes in the neutral zone. Primarily, the 0-4 emphasizes checking the wings (or the outside lanes) in the neutral zone. This allows the defensemen to be aggressive at their blue line, to stand up to the oncoming power play. Often the four penalty killers will literally form a line of defense at their blue line. Any team can use this system. A team without much speed but with good size should employ it.

1. The 0-4 is a conservative system that puts no pressure on the power play unit in the offensive zone.

2. Both forwards stay back, almost forming a line of four with the defensemen.

3. The system can be adjusted, with the forwards having either inside or outside (i.e., center of the ice or on the boards) coverage in the neutral zone.

Basic Alignment. **1**
Both forwards (P1 and P2) play back near the blue line. The defensemen (LD and RD) play their normal positions on the blue line.

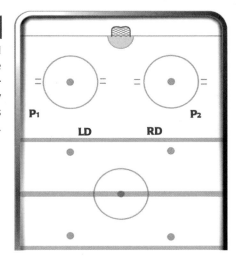

The forwards **2** each cover one side of the ice. The defensemen cover the middle. (An option is to reverse this, although the first method is recommended.) This allows the penalty-killing unit to shut off the power play beginning at the blue line.

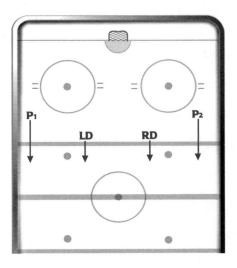

3 In the neutral zone, the forwards have the outside lanes covered. The defensemen are responsible for the middle and stand up and force the play in the neutral zone.

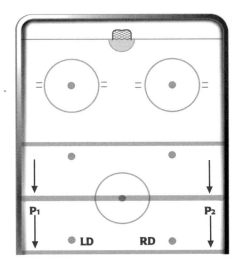

1-3

KEY POINTS

The 1-3 system combines conservatism with aggressiveness. In the offensive zone, one forward forechecks and pressures the puck while a second stays back toward the blue line. If the forechecking forward is successful in pressuring the puck, the second forward can become aggressive and join in the pressure. If the forechecking forward is not successful, the second forward is able to move to the neutral zone and assist the defensemen. This prevents any 3-on-2 or 4-on-2 breaks. In the neutral zone, the conservative forward can pressure the puck, clog up the middle or shut down one of the outside lanes. A team needs to have some fast-skating forwards to use this system. A team with size and some skating ability can use this as well.

1. The 1-3 system combines conservatism with the aggressive forechecking of one forward.

2. One forward pressures the puck, and the second forward stays back to prevent 3-on-2 breakouts. The second forward can move in if the first forward successfully pressures the puck.

3. In this system, the wings normally cover the outside lanes, and the defense covers the middle in the neutral zone. This system, however, allows some flexibility for the forwards.

Basic Alignment. One forward (P1) is deep, and the second forward (P2) stays back toward the blue line. The defensemen play their normal positions on the opponents' blue line.

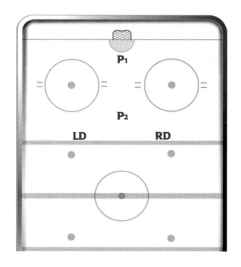

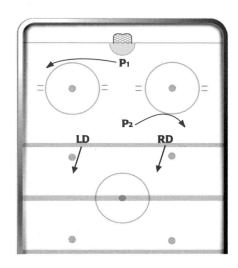

2 The forwards each cover one side of the ice. If P1 goes with the puck, P2 moves to the side away from the puck. The reverse can be used, with P2 moving to the puck and P1 moving to the opposite side. The positioning of P2 should discourage the power play unit from coming up the middle.

In the neutral **3A** zone, the forwards cover the outside lanes. The defensemen are responsible for the middle and should stand up and force the play.

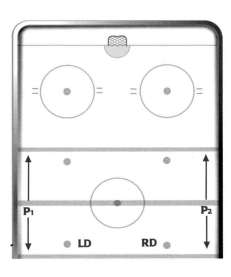

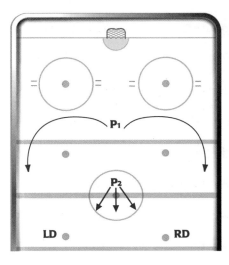

3B In the neutral zone, P2 clogs up the middle, with the objective of forcing the play toward the boards. P1, if he can get back, has the choice of moving to one side or the other. The defensemen play wide and are responsible for the outside lanes. A variation of this is to have P2 pressure the puck when it is in the middle of the ice.

2 - 2

KEY POINTS

The 2-2 is an aggressive system. It attacks the power play in the offensive zone, with the purpose of keeping it bottled up. The objective is to prevent the power play from setting up in its own end and breaking out. The two forwards exert steady pressure on the puck. They are constantly skating. Both forwards must be cognizant of their responsibility to move quickly to the defensive if the power play clears the zone. In the neutral zone, the first forward back takes an outside lane while the second comes back through the middle. Skating ability, speed and quickness are essential for this system because the attacking forwards must be able to recover immediately if the need arises. Teams without these skills cannot use it.

1. The 2-2 is an aggressive system that pressures the power play unit constantly in the offensive zone.

2. One forward goes deep to force the puck, and the other forward stays in the high slot.

3. This system demands good skating ability and hard work from the forwards.

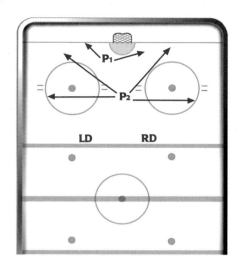

1 **Basic Alignment.** The first forward (P1) goes deep in the zone to pressure the puck. The second forward (P2) stays in the high slot. P2 is skating and is in a position to move in on the puck or to come back along either side. The defensemen (LD and RD) play their normal positions on the blue line.

The forwards can come down the boards or the middle. The objective is to have both forwards skating and able to pressure the puck. The second forward (P2) has to anticipate the reaction to the initial pressure of P1 to determine his action (Diagrams 2a and 2b).

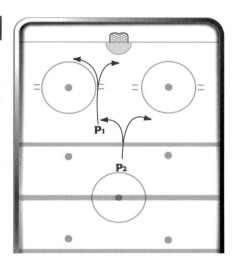

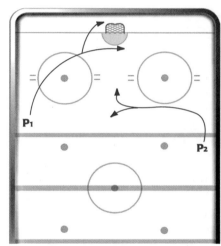

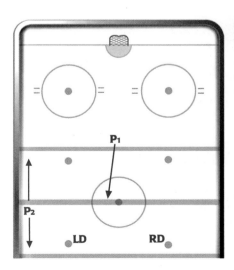

3 In the neutral zone, the first forward back (P2) takes one side. The two defensemen cover the rest of the ice. The second forward (P1), who is usually late because he was forechecking deep, comes back down the middle.

DRILLS

PENALTY KILLING IN THE OFFENSIVE AND NEUTRAL ZONES DRILLS

The following step-by-step approach can be used to teach penalty killing.

1 A complete explanation of the man-down system— its formation, objectives and options—is the initial step. Each player must know his role, the roles of the others and how the roles are related.

2 Go through the different situations slowly. Point out the possible reactions of the power play unit. A good method is to place the puck at different spots and ask the players to align themselves properly. Move the puck in different directions, and ask the players to move appropriately.

The following drills from earlier sections can be utilized to teach proper play in man-down situations:

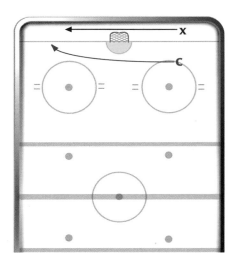

3 **Purpose:** Teach the forwards to check the puck carrier (see page 38 #1).

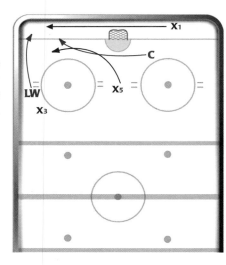

4 **Purpose:** Teach interaction between the Center and a wing (see page 38 #2).

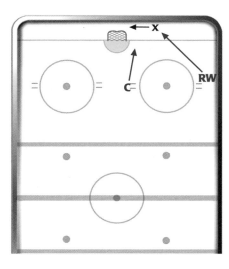

5 **Purpose:** Teach two forecheckers to pressure the puck carrier (see page 38 #4).

Purpose: Teach the two fore-checkers to react to the opposition's defense-man passing the puck to his partner. The second forechecker (C) reacts to X2's pass to X1 by moving across the ice, keeping X5 in check (see page 39).

6

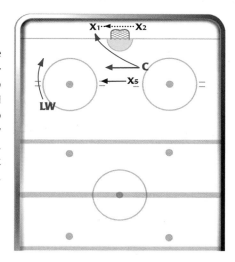

7 **Purpose**: Teach the two fore-checkers to press or attack at all times and to work as a unit. The coach dumps the puck into a corner or along the boards. A defense-man (X) retrieves the puck and attempts to make a play. The two forecheckers, starting at different spots, attack X (see page 39).

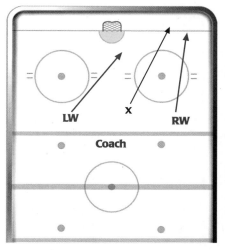

Purpose: Teach the wings close check-ing. An offensive forward without the puck skates along the boards, attempt-ing to break for the far end. The defensive player (normally a wing) stays close to the forward, preventing him from getting ahead or cutting to the middle. The checker is allowed to use his body (see page 48).

8

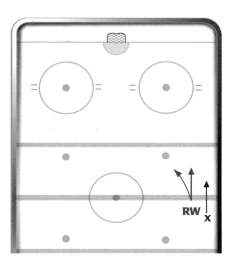

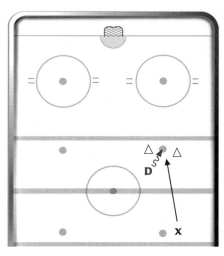

9 **Purpose**: Teach the defensemen to play the man in open ice. Two cones are placed in the neutral zone to restrict the offensive forward's mobility. The forward car-ries the puck up the ice, and the defenseman is in-structed to make his play by the blue line. The for-ward, staying within the cones, attempts to beat the defenseman or dump the puck (see page 48).

Purpose: Teach the defenseman to stand up in the neutral zone. The puck-side defenseman (RD) stands up at the red line to play the puck carrier (X), who is being pressured by the Center. The LD moves to his right, and the RW moves back to check (see page 49).

10

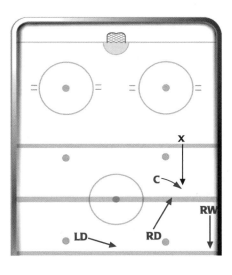

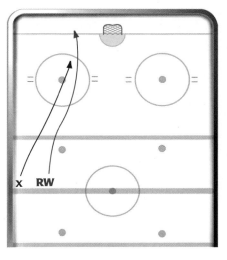

11 **Purpose**: Teach the wings proper back-checking technique (see page 58 #2).

12 Introduce the power play unit. This can be done by adding the defensemen and working on forecheck-ing, then adding the entire power play unit. This step should be done with quickness and tempo.

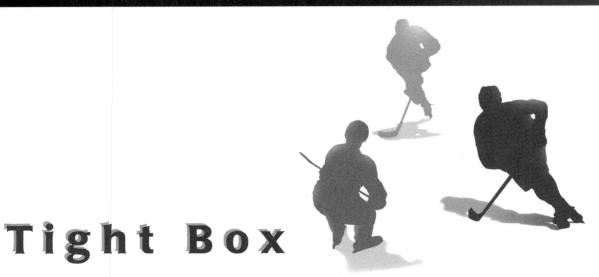

Tight Box

KEY POINTS

The Tight Box is a conservative system. It permits the power play possession of the puck in the zone but not position in front of the net or the slot area. The box has little flexibility to it. The objective is to force the power play to pass the puck outside the box and to compete for the puck when physically confronted. This system requires physical players. Courage is essential.

1. The Tight Box is a simple system that calls for discipline and toughness. Players must be willing to block shots and to play the man physically.

2. The objective is to keep the power play unit outside the box. It allows shots from the point but not from the slot area.

3. It calls for physical play to keep the opposition from getting in position for tip-ins, deflections and rebounds.

Basic Alignment. **1**A

The four penalty killers form a tight box. The box goes from the goal to no higher than the top of the face-off circle. The width of the box is no wider than face-off dots.

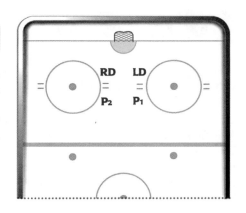

1B The Tight Box encourages the power play unit to set up around, not inside, the box.

1C It becomes the responsibility of the penalty killers to keep the forwards to the outside. It is essential that the power play unit does not get position in the slot area.

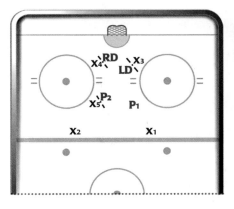

Wide Box

KEY POINTS

The Wide Box is a system that combines conservatism with aggressive play. Its objective is to discourage the opposition's defensemen from playing a prominent role in the power play. It covers a large segment of the offensive zone. The players need to have good mobility so that they can prevent the power play from moving to the inside of the box (slot area) and constantly confront the puck. The alignment is conservative; the aggressiveness comes with its mobility. All teams can use this system.

1. The Wide Box is a system that attempts to cover a large portion of the offensive zone with its box. The players require good mobility.

2. The objective is to take the points away from the power play. It attempts to eliminate shots from the points and to encourage the defensemen to pass the puck back to the forwards.

3. The defensemen are responsible for covering the slot.

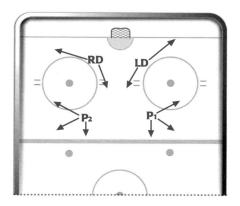

1 **A** **Basic Alignment.**
The four penalty killers form a wide box. The box attempts to cover a large section of the offensive zone. The forwards (P1 and P2) can go as far out as the blue line and as wide as the boards. The defensemen (LD and RD) can go out into the slot and as wide as the boards.

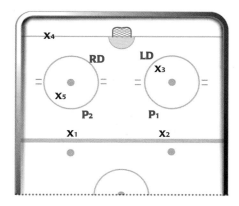

1 **B** The Wide Box discourages the power play from using the points.

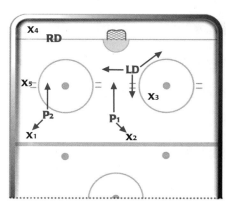

1 **C** It is the responsibility of the forwards (P1 and P2) to cover the points and also to cover the high slot. The defenseman away from the puck (LD) has to cover the slot.

Movable Box

KEY POINTS

The Movable Box is an aggressive system. It was used by the Czech national teams of the 1970s and 1980s. Its objective is to attack at every position—to attack the puck at all times. It tries to prevent the power play from setting the tempo and forces the power play unit to make plays before they are properly set up. Anticipation is the essence of this system. If one player attacks the puck, the others must cover for him and anticipate where the puck will go. Then they attack the puck there. Skating ability is crucial as well. The ability to play physically is also important.

1. The Movable Box is an aggressive system, with the penalty killers constantly moving and pressuring the puck. It attempts to pressure the players of the power play unit into moving the puck before they are ready.

2. The objective is to attack the puck and control the power play unit. It does not allow the power play to set the tempo.

3. It covers all areas: the points, slot, corners and boards. The constant motion and pressure demands coordinated movement.

Basic Alignment.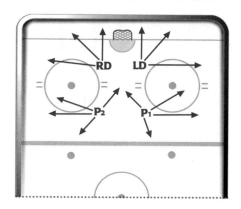

The four penalty killers form a moderate box. The box moves and goes to the puck. All four players have great liberty in their movement patterns.

The Movable Box attacks the puck.

When one player moves, the others move as well. For instance, if the defenseman (RD) goes to the puck (X4), one of the forwards (P2) moves to cover a possible outlet (X5) and the other forward (P1) drops into the slot.

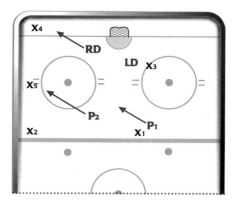

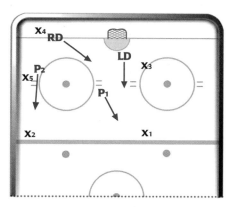

When the puck is moved (in this instance, to the point, X2), all the penalty killers have to react. P2 moves to the point, P1 moves to the other point (X1), the LD moves out into the slot, and the RD moves back to his initial position. Anticipation is needed to shut down the passing routes.

DRILLS

The following step-by-step approach can be used to teach penalty killing.

1 A complete explanation of the system—its formation, objectives and options—is the initial step. Each player must know his role, the roles of the others and how the roles are related.

2 Go through the different power play alignments that the penalty-killing unit may face. An effective method is to use stationary objects for the power play unit. Move the objects around and have the penalty-killing unit react.

The following drills from earlier sections can be utilized to teach penalty killing in the defensive zone:

3 **Purpose:** Teach the defenseman to play the man. The drill is executed by having an offensive player (X) attempt to skate out of the corner with the puck. The defenseman (RD) plays the man by keeping X to the outside and keeping himself between the puck and the net. The RD plays the man, thus separating X from the puck. An option is to add the Center to the drill. He moves in on the puck after the RD has taken control over X (see page 58).

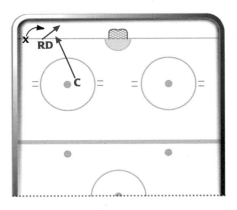

4 **Purpose:** Teach the defensemen proper position in front of the net. The off-side defenseman (LD) lines up on the far goal post. This permits him to view the entire puck-side area and not allow anyone to get behind him to the net. This positioning allows the LD to move to the opposition or the puck (see page 58).

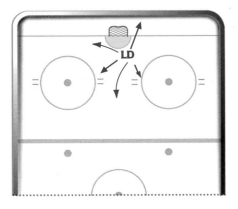

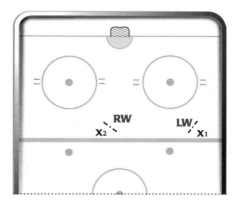

5 **Purpose:** Teach the wings proper position while covering the points. The puck-side wing (LW) must cover his point man (X1) closely by staying within a stick's length and playing a little to X1's left. This prevents X1 from moving past the LW. The off-side wing (RW) plays his point (X2) more loosely (10 to 12 feet away). The RW plays to X2's right. This prevents quick access to the high slot for X2. Both wings must watch the puck and their respective points (see page 59).

Purpose: Teach defensive role of the off-side wing. An offensive player (X3) is in the corner with the puck. X3 attempts to pass to the off-side defenseman (X2). The off-side wing (RW), positioned between the puck and X2, attempts to intercept the puck. If the puck reaches the point, the RW prevents X2 from shooting or moving to the net (see page 59). **6**

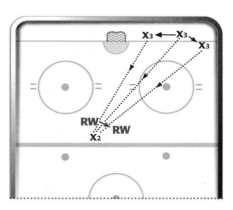

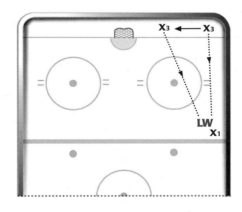

7 **Purpose:** Teach defensive role of the puck-side wing. An offensive player (X3) is in the corner with the puck. X3 attempts to pass to the puck-side defenseman (X1). The puck-side wing (LW) checks X1 closely, preventing him from either receiving the puck or moving to the puck (see page 59).

Introduce the power play unit. **8** The execution of the power play should be done with quickness and tempo.

SPECIAL TEAM PLAY

Every time the play stops, there is an opportunity to grab the tempo away from the opposition and to move onto the offensive.

Michael A. Smith

CHAPTER NINE

FACE-OFFS

F ACE-OFFS ARE AN IMPORTANT PART OF THE GAME TODAY. DURING PRACTICE, time should be spent working on offensive and defensive face-offs. Special alignments, developed to enhance scoring opportunities, should be practiced.

There are no tricks to winning face-offs. It is proper execution of the face-off fundamentals that wins face-offs. It is not just the Center who wins face-offs. Often it is the player who screens out another or the player who outfights another for the puck. Offensively, each player has a role in an attempt to get a shot at the net. Defensively, each player has a responsibility to prevent the opposition from getting a scoring opportunity.

This chapter covers offensive, defensive and neutral zone face-offs. Alignment diagrams indicate each player's responsibility, and some drills are suggested to improve face-off techniques.

Offensive Face-Offs

KEY POINTS

There are a limited number of alignments for offensive face-offs. The key is execution. The Center should be the one player who is in charge. He directs the players to the spots he thinks are best. The players must understand that each person's role is critical for every face-off.

1. The Center is responsible for everyone's proper alignment.

2. Each player must know his specific responsibility for every face-off.

3. As a unit, the purpose of each face-off must be understood.

4. Execution is critical to winning the face-off as a team.

Note: In the diagrams, the player who is marked with a square is the player to whom the puck is directed.

The LW is the shooter and lines up to the right of the circle. The RW is to screen out the opposition. The two defensemen (LD and RD) play on the blue line.

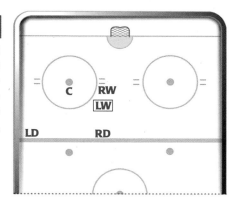

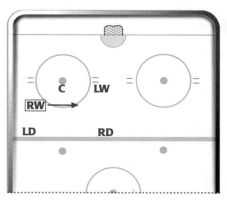

The RW is the shooter. In this alignment, the shooter plays the off-wing. He comes across the circle behind the Center. The Center draws the puck directly behind him. The LW screens out the opposition, and the two defensemen (LD and RD) play on the blue line (Diagrams 2a and 2b).

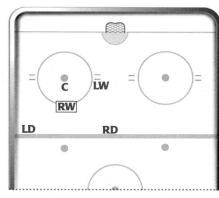

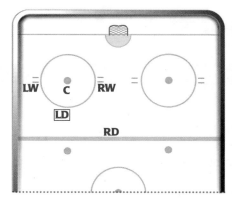

The LD is the shooter. The two wings (LW and RW) screen out the opposition. The RD plays on the blue line. The position of the shooter (LD) can vary (Diagrams 3a and 3b).

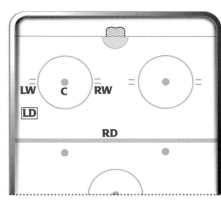

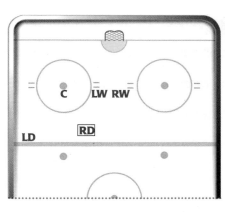

The RD is the shooter. The two wings (LW and RW) screen out the opposition. The LD plays on the blue line.

The Center goes forward with the puck. The wings (LW and RW) also go forward. The two defensemen (LD and RD) play on the blue line. The Center can direct the puck to the corner with the draw, enabling the LW to gain control of the puck.

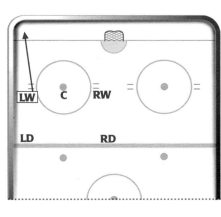

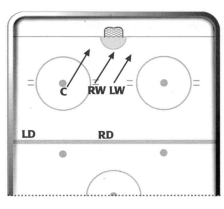

The Center can go to the net, with both wings (LW and RW) also going to the net.

Defensive Face-Offs

KEY POINTS

Members of the defensive unit should play face-offs as if they will lose them. The execution to prevent the offensive unit from making a play on the net is critical. If the defensive unit wins, it is a bonus. The Center should be the one player who is in charge. He directs the players to the spots that will counteract the offensive unit's alignment. The players must understand that their roles are critical for every face-off. Execution is essential. This section covers some general defensive roles and shows suggested alignments to counteract the face-offs diagrammed in the Offensive Face-Offs section.

1. The Center is responsible for everyone's proper alignment.

2. Players should assume that the face-off will be lost and that the team will be on the defensive.

3. Each player must know his specific responsibility for every face-off.

4. As a unit, the purpose of each face-off must be understood.

5. Execution is critical to winning the face-off.

The two wings (LW and RW) **1**A have the responsibility of checking the points and the shooter. This can be done by having the wings on both sides of the face-off circle (Diagram 1a) or on the net side (Diagram 1b). The wings usually have to fight through the opposition to get to their checks.

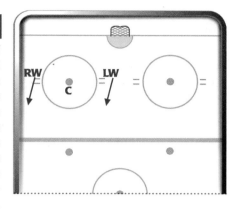

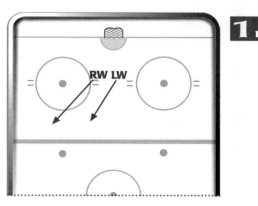

The two defensemen **2**A (LD and RD) cover the net area and the corner. There are three basic positions for the defensemen to cover their areas. The alignments (Diagrams 2a-2c) indicate the positioning and the area each player covers.

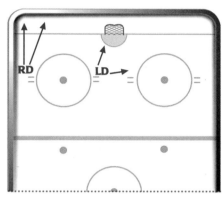

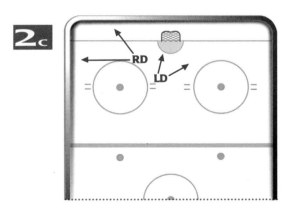

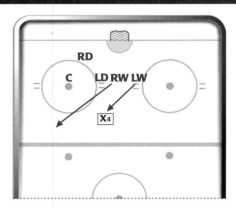

3 The shooter is the opposition's X4. The LW is responsible for him. The RW is responsible for the point. The LD picks up any player going to the net.

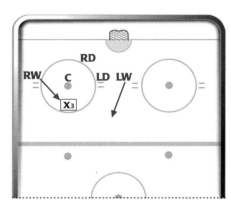

4 The opposition's off-wing (X3) is the shooter. The RW is responsible for him and, when the puck is dropped, moves to the spot where X3 picks up the puck. The LW goes to the point. The LD picks up any player going to the net.

The opposition X2 is the **5A** shooter. In this alignment, the RW checks him and comes from the net side of the face-off circle. The LW goes to the other point, and the LD picks up any player going to the net.

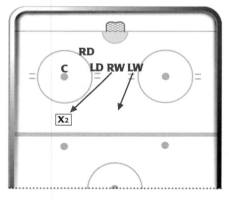

The opposition X2 is the **5B** shooter. The RW checks him and comes from the board side of the face-off circle. The LW goes to the other point, and the LD picks up any player going to the net.

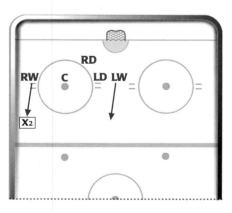

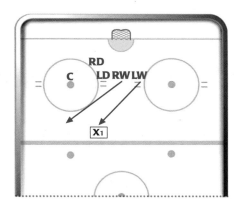

6 The opposition X1 is the shooter. The LW checks him. The RW is responsible for the other point and lines up on one side or the other of the face-off circle, depending on the opposition's alignment. The LD picks up any player on the line.

The opposition's center goes **7A** ahead with the puck. The opposition's X4 goes to the corner for the puck, the RW screens X4 out, the RD goes to the corner for the puck, and the LD picks up any player on the line.

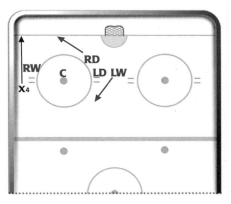

The opposition's center **7B** goes to the net with the puck. The opposition X4 and opposition X3 go to the net. The RW screens out the X3, and the LD screens out the X4. The LW goes to the point.

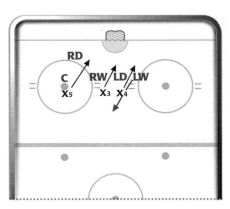

Neutral Zone Face-Offs

KEY POINTS

Time should be spent on neutral zone face-offs. Special attention should be given to defending the opposition when the face-off is lost. This brief section describes three possible defenses when the face-off is lost.

1. The Center is responsible for everyone's alignment.

2. The unit must determine in advance whether it is taking an offensive or defensive approach to the face-off.

3. Each player must know his specific responsibility for every face-off.

4. As a unit, the purpose of the face-off must be understood.

5. Execution is critical to winning the face-off.

The two wings **1** (LW and RW) can each move to a defenseman. The two defensemen (LD and RD) move up to cover the area vacated by the wings.

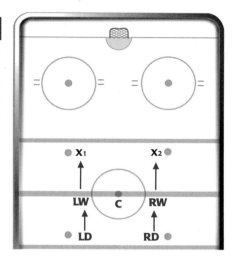

The Center goes **2** forward with the puck. The wing on the other side moves to the other defenseman. The defenseman on that side moves up to cover the area vacated by the wing. For example, if the Center goes to X2, the LW goes to X1, and the LD moves up to cover for the LW.

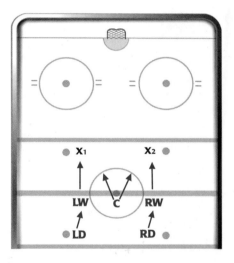

3 The Center goes to a specific defenseman, and a wing goes to the other defenseman. For example, the Center goes to X1, the RW goes to X2, and the RD moves up to cover for the RW. The LW stays with his check.

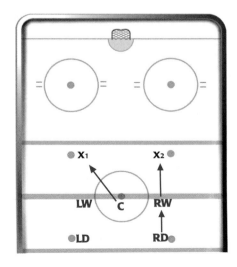

DRILLS

The following step-by-step approach can be used to teach face-off skills.

The Center works on the draw. This is done first with no opposition and then against opposition. **1**

The Center works on taking the opposition's center out of the play after the draw. Defensively, it is important that the offensive center is not allowed to go to the net. **2**

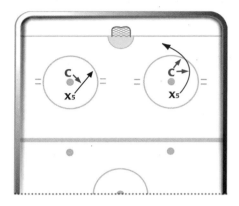

The wings practice going to **3** the points to cover the opposition's defensemen. This is done first with no opposition and then against opposition.

The wings practice going to **4** the shooter. Do this first without opposition.

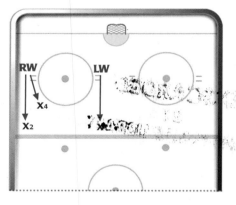

5 The wings, offensive and defensive, fight for the puck off the draw.

The defensemen practice playing **6** the man by controlling the players on the line. This is done with opposition.

The five-man unit works on **7** face-offs. This is done with no opposition. Offensively, the unit works on drawing the puck to the different shooters, getting the shot off and going to the net. Defensively, the unit works on going to different shooters and preventing the shot.

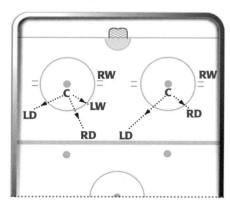

8 Step 7 with opposition added.